A WHITE MAN IN A BLACK WORLD

(CONFESSIONS OF A BENT-LEGGED PREACHER)

A MEMOIR OF

RICHARD WESLEY LYTHBERG

The cover photo shows myself, Richard Lythberg, whom you can find, a bit right of center, as the only white man in the crowd with Bishop Matthew Kwesie on my left, and my wife, Bettye, on my right. Our most notable crusades were held with this church in Obuasi, Ghana's Gold Mine City. The photo illustrates the theme of the book, "A White Man in a Black World." But the meaning also depicts our new family, my social "world," and working in black neighborhoods, teaching in black schools, and preaching in black churches.

ISBN 978-1-64492-883-7 (paperback)
ISBN 978-1-64492-884-4 (digital)

Copyright © 2019 by Richard Wesley Lythberg

All rights reserved. No part of this publication may be reproduced, distributed, or transmitted in any form or by any means, including photocopying, recording, or other electronic or mechanical methods without the prior written permission of the publisher. For permission requests, solicit the publisher via the address below.

Christian Faith Publishing, Inc.
832 Park Avenue
Meadville, PA 16335
www.christianfaithpublishing.com

Printed in the United States of America

DEDICATION

I dedicate this memoir to the Lord Jesus Christ, who makes all things possible (Matt. 6:10, KJV) and to the memory of my beloved wife and partner in ministry, Bettye Yvonne Baker Lythberg.

The beginning of romance
Bettye at Airport

This old photo, circa 1968, shows Bettye at the very beginning of our romance. Somehow, there is a red circle above her head on the original, and it looks almost like a heart. I like to think it is the beginning of her having a heart toward me. I gave her the photo, taken by myself, but she gave it back to me, as it says on the back, "To Dick, All My Love, Bettye."

CONTENTS

INTRODUCTION		7
CHAPTER 1:	FAMILY HISTORY	11
CHAPTER 2:	CHILDHOOD	35
CHAPTER 3:	CONVERSION AND CALL TO MINISTRY	42
CHAPTER 4:	LIFE AFTER CONVERSION	48
CHAPTER 5:	EDUCATION	61
CHAPTER 6:	SECULAR AND CHRISTIAN WORK	71
CHAPTER 7:	THE MIRACULOUS BAPTISM OF THE HOLY SPIRIT	115
CHAPTER 8:	BETTYE!	132
CHAPTER 9:	HEALING AND OTHER MIRACLES	147
CHAPTER 10:	"ANGELS" AND "DEMONS"	156
CHAPTER 11:	AFRICA—A MIXED BAG	164
CHAPTER 12:	THEY DIDN'T WANT TO COME HERE	174
CHAPTER 13:	BETTYE'S LAST DAYS	185
EPILOGUE: TO YOUR HEALTH!		191
CONCLUSION: TO YOUR ETERNITY!		197
BIBLIOGRAPHY		199

INTRODUCTION

When I first thought of writing my memoir, it was to be just for my own "amazement" or "amusement,"—i.e., to analyze my life to see if I did anything right, and/or where I failed and could have done better. But then I thought, perhaps someone else might benefit from my mistakes and even successes.

I must begin with two disclaimers: (1) the title, *A White Man in a Black World*, does not mean I lived my whole life that way, neither does it mean I lived most of my life in Africa. Nor does it mean, of course, that the USA is a *black* country. What it does mean is that, probably, sometime in my late teens, I would sometimes take a bus in Chicago to 63rd and Loomis, and then catch the L (elevated train), which went right through the black neighborhoods, revealing their backyards, where I would see people on my way downtown. God must have been speaking to me because I remember thinking, *Someday, I'm going to help these people*. But I quickly forgot that thought until it came back to me years later.

And in college, I began having more and more fellowship with black people, until I worked in black neighborhoods, taught in a black school, conducted a club with black gang boys, loved and married a black woman, and finally, spending several years as a missionary in Africa. As I write, my beloved wife of almost forty-seven years, Bettye, is now in heaven, having gone to the loving arms of Jesus, after much suffering. I have no doubt she is there with the Lord because the Apostle Paul says in the Bible, "*Absent from the body is to be present with the Lord*" (2 Cor. 5:8), and the penitent thief on the cross said, "*Lord, remember me, when you come into your kingdom.* And Jesus answered, "Assuredly I say to you, today you will be with Me in Paradise" (Luke 23:43). So I rejoice and have peace with God, knowing where she is!

The second disclaimer is that I hate to call myself "a bent-legged preacher," but I must admit that is what you could call me. (To the best of my understanding, a "bent-legged preacher" is a black phrase for a preacher who is, perhaps, uneducated or somehow lacking in the ability to get his message adequately understood by his audience. At least it could be true of me. That is what Bettye called me, because she felt I was preaching over the heads of the people, in mentioning famous white preachers whom they did not know.

This, then, is the story of a very ordinary person. Why do I call these memoir *A White Man in a Black World*? It's because that is the most *unusual* thing about my story. My black world is now my black family—our four children (including my stepdaughter); our grandchildren and great-grandchildren; and our African American relatives, brothers- and sisters-in law, cousins, and nephews and nieces. Besides this, as I said, I spent several years teaching in largely African American schools, and more than twenty-one years working for the state of Illinois Job Service, seeking to place (mainly) African Americans in jobs or job training, also as an adjudicator (small time judge) handling their cases for unemployment compensation.

I had just one brother. When he was dying from cancer, I went to the hospital to cast out the spirit of incurable disease, joining hands with his family around the bed. Even though his own pastor had given him up to die that night, we prayed, and he *lived* another year or so! And perhaps, he would have lived longer, if he could have embraced the healing message I tried to bring him.

Although I love my white family (the families of my brother's five children, and their children and grandchildren) I don't see them very often, because most of my time is taken up by my *black* family. You might say this is my social life now. But since this is also my memoir, I will begin with my ancestors, parents, grandparents, and other relatives. This is the story of a "maverick" (a different breed of horses—in my case, a different type of person) who sought God for some seven years before finding the full assurance of salvation and then a total of almost eleven years before receiving the great baptism of the Holy Spirit. It is also the story of a white man and a black woman finding *love* that goes beyond racism "through many trials and tribulations," as Bettye would later write, and the fact that "opposites attract." And I learned to tell other couples that "if we can make it, *anyone* can!"

In writing my memoir, my purpose is to show what it means to become a Christian and the problems of working out Christian character—in my case, in an interracial marriage, but not to the exclusion of any other race.

I will deal with my education and spiritual highlights; and then, my life in the black community, dating and marrying my black wife, problems in the marriage and family relationship, in the Christian ministry, and finally, missionary work in Africa, and the last years as caregiver for my beloved wife and her suffering, as she developed many maladies, requiring her to spend much time in doctor's offices, hospitals, and nursing homes, ending in a hospice, where she died at eighty years of age, finally ending in a beautiful home-going funeral. She is now with her Lord in heaven! Now, my last years are being spent with an assignment from God, as a writer.

So I hope you will enjoy and profit from this story, which I dedicate to *the glory of God* and the blessing of many, who can learn, not only from our mistakes, but from the blessings we received from God. And may it strike a blow toward eliminating racism in our country and in the world. Amen.

(One last precaution—in some cases, I may mention people without disclosing their names to avoid any probability of attaching unfavorable publicity to their names and character.)

CHAPTER 1

FAMILY HISTORY

I was always told that my ancestors were Swedish, from the island of Gotland, off the coast of Sweden, in the Baltic Sea. But my great-great-great-grandfather on my father's side of the family came from Wismar, Germany. I hate to say so, but there were rumors that he was a pirate. He was a very wealthy man, a sea captain, named Joachim David Muchau. As a child, I used to hear people talk about *Gouba Muchau* (*gouba* means old man, or perhaps, elder).

My mother, Josephine Helena Wickstrom Lythberg, who was born and raised near Visby, Gotland, used to tell me it was known as a place where pirates buried their treasure. But the facts I got about Capt. Muchau are from my Aunt Hilma, my father's oldest living sister, at that time, in 1964, who wrote a nine-page history about my grandmother's (Blomberg) family.

Muchau had several ships, one of which he sold to the German government in their war. He also loaned them money. He owned lime kilns, two harbors, and two estates (one for his servants) in Gotland. He was a member of the Hanseatic League. He had a room that was always kept locked, filled with beautiful, precious things, including a long sock, filled with golden "ducats" (the money of that time).

He married an eighteen-year-old heiress from Germany, named Victoria Von Calysendorf. She was beautiful and brought another fortune to her husband. They soon had a little baby girl, but then the devil stepped in. One fine morning, she happened to see her husband making love with the baby's governess in the garden. It was more than she could take. Unfortunately, she committed suicide.

But the Captain, then married the governess who tried her best to make up for the young mother's tragic death by sending her child to the best school, where she learned the arts, horseback riding and became an expert pianist. But alas, Muchau's lavish parties and carousing every weekend dwindled his wealth to the place that he forced his daughter to sign over to him her mother's wealth. Muchau married again and had another daughter to whom he left his remaining wealth, plus that which rightly belonged to his first daughter, Anna Maria Muchau Skotte, as she married a Swedish sea captain. It is said, however, that she never spoke against her father.

It was Anna Maria's daughter, Maria Margretta Skotte, my Aunt Hilma's grandmother (my great-grandmother) who told her these stories and facts. Aunt Hilma said of her grandmother, whom she loved dearly, "Grandmother was a wonderful woman in every respect; considered severe by many. Yes, severe she was when she had occasion to deal with some wrongdoing, gentle and kind when she needed to give help and comfort to the sick, as she very often did. You could always depend on Grandma. Neighbors all around came to her to help solve their problems and always found her ready."

She was born in 1828 and died in 1909. Aunt Hilma says, "She was a woman of great endurance and determination." She married Daniel Henrie Blomberg, a shipbuilder and ship's carpenter. They had seven children, including Annette, my grandmother, born in 1852 and died in 1950. While her husband was away at sea, Great-Grandmother studied medicine at Stockholm, the capital of Sweden. She received a diploma and practiced medicine to help support her large family.

In her early or midforties, the family took a small sailing vessel and moved to London, England. (Aunt Hilma does not tell us why they left Gotland, but no doubt, they thought they could do better in England.) All the Blomberg children were musical and played instruments. Fred, one of the sons, played in a large band, including six drums and a big Prussian bass drum. They played such songs as "God Save the Queen" and "God Bless the Prince of Wales." Fred's children also played drums, and Fred played coronet, flute, and concertina, besides. When Fred moved to Chicago, he organized a Salvation Army Band in Roseland.

All of Uncle Fred's' children were skillful in various ways. As a hobby, Fred himself made a fine model of the small boat, which took them to London. It had all the small details, e.g., bunk beds, galley, etc. One son, Julius, was a skilled cabinetmaker. He became a Chicago policeman and was killed on duty while taking a child across a track on a foggy day. Henrie, another brother, built violins, also a large pipe organ for a north side church. He directed a large choir in the Mission church, which he brought to the little church where the family attended in Hegewisch, Illinois, south of Chicago. They were trying to raise money for Great-Grandmother's trip to London, at age sixty, to help her son, Anton, who was in a hospital for crippling arthritis. They raised only enough for her fare to London. But she went anyway and called on the Swedish consul, who gave her all the assistance he could. She rented a few rooms and took her son out of the hospital. He only lived a few months, but at least, his mother was with him in his last days.

Aunt Hilma lived seven more years after writing her historical account of the Blomberg family, and we are all indebted to her for that. I appreciate it very much, particularly her telling of the many hardships she went through in her life. It brought tears to my eyes, as I never heard her talk about these things in person. Although she did not talk a great deal about God, as you will read, she trusted in God in the nearly impossible situations she faced. No doubt, she attended the Emerald Avenue Swedish Baptist Church, on Chicago's south side, with the family and, in later years, Sunday school and church services at the Salem Baptist

Church in Evergreen Park. So I would hope she trusted in Jesus, our Savior, and is now in heaven.

My paternal grandparents and their family lived in London for five or six years somewhere between the 1870s and 1880s. Great-Grandmother Skötte kept a boardinghouse for sailors when they came in on leave from their ships. This is how my grandmother, Annette Blomberg, met my grandfather, Alexander Lythberg, who was a chef on a large ocean liner.

A funny story is told of their courting days. Annette was working at a corset factory. Alexander often met her after work. One day, her three brothers wanted to go with him, and they were in a jovial mood, laughing hilariously, when Annette came out of the factory door. But her boss came out at the same time, and being not amused to see her walking away with four men, he called her into the office. Although she told him that one of them was the man to whom she was engaged, and the others were her brothers, he was skeptical and said, "If you wish to work here, see that this does not happen again." Grandmother was quite humiliated, but everyone just joked with her about it.

While they lived in London, they saw all the noted places and great buildings but also the many slums where men and women drank and caroused. Grandmother Annette said, "I never saw women sink so low as those who hung around the docks waiting for a ship to land."

So my grandparents were married in the Poplar Church in All Saints Parish, as listed in census, in London, but later moved back to Visby, the capital of Gotland, where they built the only stone house there. Aunt Hilma, by the way, was quite an inspiration to me as a schoolteacher, her whole life, until age eighty-five. (More on that later.) Here is Hilma's tribute to her father, whom I never saw, as he died when my father, his son, was only six years old:

Hilma again says, "I'd like to tell you something about my father. His father died when he was quite young. His mother was left with two sons, William, who was a few years younger than Alexander, my father...to support herself and children, she kept a bakery in Visby. Her two sons received more than average education and went through high school. When I was in High School I could always go to father for help in the solution of a difficult problem. He learned languages and higher mathematics. Quiet, kind, helpful in every way. Mother never took the initiative in solving problems, but everything went to father. When we asked a privilege, we were always told, 'Ask your father.' He often came home with lovely materials, which mother made into dresses for us, as she was an expert seamstress."

I remember two other things Aunt Hilma told me about Grandfather Lythberg. He went to a Pentecostal revival meeting one night and came home and threw away all his pipes and tobacco. (I would say that Grandfather Alex died about 1899 or 1900, since he is said to have died when my father was six years old. So this occurred before the Great Azusa Street Revival, beginning in 1906.) There were movements called Pentecostal, mostly growing out of Methodism, inspired by John Wesley, but also from Baptist groups as early as 1886.

The second thing was that there was one "colored" family in their neighborhood with whom the Lythberg children used to play. They even stayed overnight once, but at this point, Grandfather said, "This has gone a little too far." It reminds me of Carter Woodson, in his book, *The Mis-education of the Negro*, telling of white men being placed as president of Negro colleges, who would not allow their students in their houses. Little did Grandfather know that one day his grandson would break the color line he was upholding, as a child of his times.

Let me say, at this point, that I was told that my nephew, Bill Jr., recently did some research on our name *Lythberg* and found that it came from a man named *Lyth,* who married a lady named *Berg,* thus *Lythberg.* My father used to tell me it meant "*iron mountain,*" perhaps meaning "*strong or sturdy mountain.*"

Aunt Hilma also mentions her grandfather, my great-grandfather, Henrie Blomberg, as a tall, strong, broad-shouldered man, who had served in the Swedish military. Once, his friends tried to play a trick on him. They emptied his toolbox and filled it with heavy scrap metal. They dared him to try to lift it. Imagine their surprise when he pushed them out of the way, picked up the heavy tool chest, and walked away. He was said to be a Bible-quoting man, with a long white beard, who would sit and play hymns on his violin at night.

It was about 1881 when the whole family decided to move to the United States. They first visited their relatives from the Muchau family in New Jersey. But when my grandfather saw there was no work there, they moved on to Chicago and settled in Pullman, then a thriving suburb with a large car shop. "It was not difficult for father to obtain work, as both he and mother spoke perfect English, having learned it in their years in London."

My Lythberg grandparents had nine children (again, as listed in the census record I recently saw), but at least, one died in infancy and one at the age of five. Aunt Hilma tells about her sister, one year older than her: "Matilda Clara…was a gay, laughing, beautiful girl with curly auburn hair. I was plain, serious and an avid reader. She was a grade ahead of me in school, but when I was in seventh grade I was permitted to try eighth, so now we were both in the same grade. I was then twelve years old. She never bothered to do her assignments, but when I went to bed, copied them from me. We had many battles about this, but strange to say, my sister won out. It was not that she wasn't talented, but just wouldn't exert herself. In this same year, she won the Daily News Medal for an essay on Patriotism. We were very proud of this.

"Then came the day, she turned around to me and whispered, 'I'm sick. I'm going home.' She walked up to Miss Hunter, our teacher, asked to be excused and, flashing a gay smile at the room, left. When I came home she had a raving fever and died in three days. The illness baffled the two doctors who were called in… In later years they diagnosed it as spinal Cerebral Meningitis. School was dismissed the day of her funeral; six classmates dressed in white were pallbearers. She was dressed in her white confirmation dress. And looked like an angel. At that time, we attended a small Mission Church, where she played the organ every Sunday. The last Sunday she attended, she played and sang for the first time, 'God Be with You till We Meet Again.' This song was sung and played at her funeral. Even to this day, when I hear it, I think of my beautiful older sister, who left us when she was so full of life and gaiety."

AUNT HILMA

"The Minister's sermon was 'The Hour Has Come.' Now I was the oldest and had somehow to fit into my sister's place. As I said then, and many times later, there was always a baby in the house. I never could go anyplace unless I took the baby with me. I can remember sitting under a tree, with the baby beside me, trying to study. I began to resent this and it seems that my mother was always saying, 'You can go, if you take the baby!'"

Since they lived in Hegewisch, Illinois, south of Chicago, Aunt Hilma goes on to tell how she did not have the $2.75 for a train ticket to south Chicago to attend high school, as her great ambition was to be a teacher. She had to walk several miles "through dense woods, leaving home at 7 o'clock.... I have often thought of that lonely walk through the woods and what might have happened to a young girl, but God watched over me." She could not afford a biology book but tried to borrow one from her friends, when they were not using it. But she says, "The four years passed quickly...and graduation day came. My average for the four years was 93%, so I did not have to take an examination to Teacher's College.

"Now dark days came again. I had graduated from Teacher's College and was just starting to cadet, before being permanently assigned as a teacher. Father became ill and for many months was out of work. Debts piled up. He died just as I was first assigned, leaving no insurance. I was then eighteen years old, faced with greater responsibilities than an adult could cope with. I was the head of the family. Mother withdrew in a shell. I remembered how I hated to come home at night, as all I could see was her tear stained face. 'Everything was up to Hilma.' I took a position at

Hamline School evenings, teaching adult classes. I worked day and night and finally all our debts were cleared away.

"I was first assigned in Chicago Lawn and I had no sooner started when I had typhoid fever. My life was despaired of, was out of school for three months, so now I was back where I was before. But God took care of that. That was about the time Grandfather died at our house. Well, it sure is by adversities we receive strength, when days are darkest, God steps in with help and comfort. This was true in my case."

***

As was already noted, Aunt Hilma was a teacher until the age of eighty-five and loved her profession. As I taught a few years myself, I asked her for advice. I asked her what she did about discipline problems. She "floored me" as she said, "I didn't have any discipline problems." She explained, a boy who threw a spitball stayed after school or at recess making five hundred spitballs. (He didn't throw any more, after that!)

To continue the story of her life, Hilma says, "In 1909 I met Olaf Welin. We were both attracted to each other at first sight. Married December 28, 1910. I kept on teaching. We built a lovely home at 114th and Wentworth.... In 1919 Joyce was born, a happy child and idolized by both of us. Her first Christmas was a memorable one. We had a large tree, which she watched continuously and was fascinated by the bright lights. Olaf said, 'I don't think there is anyone in the world who is happier than we are today.' We had all the relatives over for 'Smorgasbord' [note, a Swedish meal setting, with a variety of foods] on Christmas Eve."

Then she tells about another tragedy in her life, her strong, healthy husband developed an ulcer; and although he was careful about his diet, peritonitis set in and he died. Her daughter, Joyce, was only one year old. Hilma remembered the funeral message directed to her, "Your friends can comfort and help you just so far, but down to the depths of your sorrow, you must travel alone. This will show what you are and may God give you strength to meet your new life."

"This He has done," she says, "In the darkest days, when Olaf had just died, I could only feel like going on when I thought of my responsibility to her [her daughter] and she needed me." She went back to a very successful teaching career, with my grandmother taking care of her baby. She took "many wonderful trips... was a delegate of the IEA and NEA [teachers' organizations] went to Columbus, Seattle, Alaska, Atlanta, San Francisco, Denver and in 1933 to Los Angeles, where I was Miss Chicago."

Their daughter, Joyce, married her high school sweetheart during World War II, and they had four children. Joyce recently died, in her nineties. I remember visiting them when her boys were young and showing at least one of them the "Wordless Book," which explains the way of salvation, and they were very interested. I hope they are following the Lord, as I have not seen them since, as I was estranged from my family when they learned I wanted to marry a woman of another race. In fact, years later, when Bettye and I were travelling with our children, we were near Joyce's home in Florida. I called and asked if we could see her or if I could see her. She said, "I don't think that is a good idea."

However, I did call her some years later, a year or two before she died, and she did speak more amiably to me.

***

Most people are closer to their mothers than their fathers because, of course, she is the one who brought you into the world and nurtured and cared for you and largely brought you up. This is not to neglect the importance of fathers, which are so lacking today—one of the reasons we have divorces, broken families, and children suffering from missing their fathers. It is a reason for crime, poverty, and women working hard, trying to be both mother and father to their children. My book, *Men's Manual for Holiness, With Particular Reference to Sexual Purity*, deals with this very subject—*that every child deserves and needs both a father and mother.*

My mother, Josephine Helena Wickstrom Lythberg, grew up on a farm, near the city of Visby, Gotland, an island, as I have said, off the coast of Sweden in the Baltic Sea. She had several brothers—all were sailors, and all could swim like fishes. But she herself could not swim. Probably because she had to do the housework and farmwork while her brothers were away at sea. I think she had a sister, or two, but I have no records, telling their names, if any.

She used to tell me, when there were storms at sea, how the women and children would come to the sea shore or harbor to wait for the ships to come in, hoping against hope, that their husbands, sons, and brothers would come in. This made me think how we ought to be waiting and looking for the blessed hope, the coming of our Lord and Savior, Jesus Christ! (See 1 Thessalonians 4:16,17; Titus 2:13.)

She would not like me to tell you, but she only went to the fourth grade in school. Again, it was because she was needed to do farm chores. It must have been hard times when they heard of the new land of opportunity—*America!* At least two of her brothers had preceded her to the new country across the sea. My uncle John had gone to east Chicago, Indiana, and was working at the nearby steel mill. Anthony went to California, apparently as a sailor but, later, somehow, drowned in the Pacific Ocean, off the coast of California. I never heard any details of his death

I know it was heart-wrenching for Josephine to leave her mother. She was then only eighteen and accompanied by her nephew, Olaf Carlson, who was a few years younger than her. They often talked about their ocean journey years later. The waves were so high, like mountains, that they both got "sea-sick" and went to bed. Finally, they docked at Ellis Island, and Josephine heard her first two English words—"Sit down!"

But despite her scanty education, she learned quickly; so that a few years later, she read whole books in English. I was in elementary school, I remember, when she took the test to become an American citizen. (Of course, she passed it.) Somehow, she was hired as a cook by wealthy Jewish people on the north shore of Lake Michigan in the Chicago area. I am not surprised, for all my life, I knew her as a wonderful cook, preparing Swedish meatballs, deviled eggs, and many other special dishes for holidays and other events. For Christmas, she made all kinds of cookies and other desserts, including pumpkin and mincemeat pies, and fruitcakes. It was not unusual for her to send me down to Levey's neighborhood grocery store for a "pound of ground round steak," as she prepared supper.

I'm not sure how my father got to know my mother, but it may have been the same way his father met grandmother. I heard a lot about "Auntie Bennett," who ran a boardinghouse, and as Swedish immigrants, it is very possible that they met there. The two families may have been acquainted, as they both came from Visby, Gotland. But remember that Annette Blomberg, my grandmother, who married Alexander Lythberg, came to America many years earlier. Therefore, Percy Lythberg (my father) was born here in Hegewisch, Illinois.

I was told that soon after they were married, Josephine was making more money than Percy. Here is how that happened. Josephine got a job at a dress company. At lunchtime or on breaks, she would talk on the telephone, doodling and drawing flowers while she talked. Someone saw her drawings and showed them to Mr. Scott, the owner, who liked them and gave Josephine the job as a dress designer, with a larger salary than my father, at that time. Later in her life, Josephine would make boutonnieres and other cloth-flower corsages, which were very lifelike, and sell them. She loved flowers and horses and said, had she been a man, she would have liked to have been a carpenter.

In about seventh grade, I had a classmate who delivered papers after school, and he liked to stop by our house often, although we did not take the newspaper. I asked him why he stopped at our house so often, and he replied that he liked to hear my mother's accent. I was surprised, as I was used to her way of talking and didn't know that she had an accent. She did pronounce, for instance, the word *room* more like *rum*.

She was a good mother and loved us all very much. And she never whipped or spanked us, however, that I can recall.

Percy Axel Clarence Matthew Lythberg was my father's name. At least that is what he told me. He was probably raised as much by his sister, Hilma, as by his mother. His father died when he was only six years old, and I think, he somewhat resented Hilma mothering him. But at the same time, he respected her. Let's face it. She did bring the family through some hard times. I was born in the depression of 1929, and my father was out of work. So I seldom saw him as he was out looking for a job every day. He would leave home before I got up and came back after I was in bed. The story is told that once he got a job as a clothes salesman and sold one hundred suits of clothes at Miller, Indiana. In those days, they used large pieces of cloth for samples. My mother would take and sew them together and make clothes for my brother and me. But for Mom, there was a time when she had only one dress to her name.

I believe it was in 1933 that Dad was hired by the Sawyer Biscuit Company to place cookies in stores. I remember that year very well. I was four years old. It was the year of the World's Fair in Chicago, and we took in visitors to stay overnight, sleeping on our living room floor, for a dollar a night. I remember wearing red, white, and blue clothes at the Fair. People could take rides up in the air, over the Fair. I couldn't understand it at all. And I think it was Battling Nelson, the boxer from Hegewisch, my father's birthplace, who would pay people a big prize, if they could lift him off the ground. But he would touch them somewhere on their neck (I suppose, paralyzing them), and no one could lift him off the ground, small, though he was.

Someone said about Lovie Smith, a recent coach of the Chicago Bears, that he *had* to be tough, with a name like that. That must have been the same with my father, as Percy was considered a sissy name. He must have gone to the gym and learned to box. I don't know the details, but he spoke of boxing semipro, as far away as Kansas City. He went by the name of "Young Moran," I think, referring to Pal Moran, a well-known boxer in those days. I have seen him spar with Ed Belyea, Joyce's husband, who worked with him for a while, and there was no doubt Dad could box. When we were little kids, he would show us his biceps, and we thought they were the biggest in the world. But they were not, we learned later. He boxed at 133 pounds, lightweight, and was tall, five eleven, slim, but broad shouldered. I was told my grandmother got very angry when his boxing comrades came around and asked, "Where's Moran?"

Daddy was not a braggart, at all; but later, when he was working as a supervisor for the Salerno-Megowen Biscuit Company, he told us of once hitting one of his salesmen in the jaw and knocking him out. I knew the man, too. He was rather large and robust. But this was completely out of character for him. He never whipped or spanked us (my brother and I). He did threaten to use his razor strap to whip us, and we were afraid. But he never did it!

Both my mother and my father were born in 1893, and I believe they were married in 1923, at about thirty years of age. He and his sister, my aunt Matilda, when they were children, used to give recitations out on the streets and sing songs for money. They called them Sunshine and Sunshine's sister. She would talk about "the Face on the Ballroom Floor," and he "the Kid's Last Fight." I mention this because, later, the government either banned boxing or were threatening to do so, and Dad would give speeches about boxing that the boxers were "gentle giants" and not a threat to anyone, etc.

All in all, he was a good father but didn't talk to us, my brother and I, much. He was afraid of heights, and I must have inherited it, but fought against it. Any work around the roof had to be done by me, and even window washing, he did not do. The one thing he was good at was electric work, for which I always had to "hold the flashlight." It used to exasperate me because I would rather do something other than just "hold the flashlight."

Of the few things he did tell us, one was "If you mean to do a thing, and mean to do it, really, never let it be by halves, but do it, fully, freely," which reminds me of the wisdom of Solomon in Ecclesiastes 9:10, "*Whatsoever thy hand findeth to do, do it with thy might*" (KJV). He also stressed 'Plan your work and work your plan,' which is good advice, but we must be careful that our plan is from God. (See James 4:13-17) The only other advice I remember from him was this, "The best exercise is pushing yourself away from the table. You should always feel like you could eat a little more, when you leave the table." My guess is that this wisdom came from the fact he had to make the weight, I believe, of 133 pounds to fight as a lightweight. He did tell us how to throw a punch from the shoulder. Dad also talked about two- inch punches. He did not explain this punch, but as he demonstrated it, it would seem that though the punch was only two inches, the boxer hit the opponent, as if trying, with all his power, to punch right through him.

Two books I inherited from him, which have disappeared by this time—(1) some good spiritual advice, by F. B. Meyers, an old British or South African Divine; and (2) a book about exercise and posture, etc., some of which, I practiced for years.

My mother handled the finances, but if there was anything that displeased him, you could hear my father, down in the basement, grumbling over his tools.

My mother and father were both baptized (by immersion) at fifty years of age. For years, they had sent us to Sunday school but did not go themselves. We went to the Foster Park Baptist Church. Rev. Adam Baum (Atom Bomb), who was born in Germany, was our pastor then. If I didn't go to Sunday school, I didn't feel right. I would get a headache. Later, in my twenties, if I went to the movies, I felt like I was in the wrong place. I believed my mother was saved but was not so sure about Dad. Years later, he drove me to Oklahoma, where I took my first pastorate. Later, I wrote him a letter, pretty much, telling him he was not saved. He wrote me back saying that maybe he believed more sincerely than I thought. I never talked to him about the subject again. But he did love to listen and watch the broadcasts of Billy Graham, the evangelist. And when he died, there appeared to be a smile on his face! I trust I'll see him in heaven!

William Clarence Lythberg was my big brother, twenty-two months older than me. Our aunt, Hannah Marie, the "black sheep" of the family, but perhaps, the aunt who loved us the most, called us the "savages" because we were always fighting. They would make us sit on chairs in different rooms to break up our fights. But after sitting apart a little while, we were the best of friends again. Later, we were great sports fans. He was for the Cubs, and I, the White Sox. We would listen to the Bears football games and knew all about Cecil Isbell and Don Hutson of the Green Bay Packers and, of course, Sid Luckman and all the Bears players. As soon as Bill got a job as a young man, he bought a season's pass to all the Bears games. Bill was good in all sports. He could hit home runs in softball (sixteen inches) and played third base or left field, later becoming an excellent hesitation pitcher. (And I was so proud of him!) He used to beat his pal, Roy Aiken, in basketball, but Roy made the Calumet High School team and Bill did not, probably because Roy was taller.

When that new invention, television, came out, about 1950, Bill used his first good pay, working in the stock yards, to buy a nine-inch TV set, one of the first in our neighborhood, and we all enjoyed it. Before that, we listened to the radio and used our imagination.

Our school did not have much of a track team, but Bill got all the measurements somewhere and made what looked like a perfect hurdle and practiced jumping it, but never followed through because, as I said, there was no organized team behind him. We played scrub football and even got our parents to buy us shoulder pads and helmets. But in the fall, when we were not watching our Calumet High School team practice, we played "Touch Football." I remember, in eighth grade, when we were dismissed for recess, the boys in our class would run as fast as we could to the sidewalk on 86th Street. (Foster Park School was between 85th and 86th streets) because the last one there was always "it" when we played tag. Every day, I would tell myself, "I must run faster," but I was seldom "it."

In all my spare time in school, I would try to diagram plays for our touch football games. I liked to be on Bill's team because, from watching our high school team practice, he knew just what to do as a passer. He would say, "Go out five steps, and the ball will be there," etc., and it would be just as he said. I had great confidence in him that he would throw the ball just as he said.

Another thing Bill did was to make a heavy punching bag, I think, out of an old duffel bag he got somewhere. He filled it with sand, and it was very heavy. The Golden Gloves boxing tournaments were popular in Chicago in those days, and we were going to enter the Golden Gloves. I would hit that heavy bag very hard, and I got to thinking I didn't want anyone to hit me that hard. So I guess I chickened out. Somehow, we never did enter the Golden Gloves!

Bill and his pal, Roy, went downtown and applied for the Marine Corps when they were still in high school. At the end of all the tests, the recruiter said, "Okay, you made it! You can leave tonight on the train for Parris Island, South Carolina." It was 1945, during World War II.

Bill and Roy said, "We are still in school. We haven't graduated yet!"

"Is that so important?" asked the recruiter. "Well. I guess you have to wait, then." But they did leave for Parris Island as soon as they graduated.

It was very rough training. Bill weighed only 135 pounds when he left. After basic, he came home weighing about 165! The marines had built him up. He went back to Camp Lejeune, North Carolina. There, they told them they would invade Tokyo, as we were fighting the Japanese at that time. But then the "atom bomb" was invented and perfected by Einstein and others and was dropped on two Japanese cities, and the war was soon over. Bill was stationed at Tientsin, China. When he was discharged and came home, he weighed 180 pounds.

Meanwhile, Bill had taught me all the rules for high school wrestling when I was still in eighth grade, and in my sophomore year, I went out for the team. I weighed 119 pounds and wrestled in the 115-pound class. I gave the first-string senior a good fight, but I couldn't quite beat him. But I got ringworm of the scalp (I suppose, from the wrestling mats) and had to quit the team.

In those days, my mother had to scrape the scabs off my head every hour, and it was very painful. Later, I had a nervous stomach and a thyroid problem, bringing my weight down to only 90 pounds, as I began my senior year in high school. Bill would wrestle and fight with me, throwing me around, trying to toughen me up. I was not angry at him, but I felt very ashamed. Although he was two years older than me, we had grown up together, and I was **never** afraid of him. I could hold my own. But now, he weighed about 180 pounds, and I was only 90 pounds, one half of his weight. And I was ashamed, but not mad, as I knew he was trying to do me good. But I didn't know what else to do.

Before we leave my brother, Bill, I would like to tell you about his later years. He was married young, at age twenty-three, to Joan Dornan, after graduating from the University of Illinois. I believe he majored in business or accounting. Anyway, he worked many years for the Wilton Cake Company. He was their business manager.

Bill was an usher at the time, in our Baptist Church, and he would see this young lady come in and sit near the aisle. Bill would say, "I hope no one sits next to her." And one Sunday, that was true. He got to sit next to her, and the rest is history! They were married and had five children—four boys and one girl, Kristine, and I really don't know how many grandchildren. I have tried to keep up with them, particularly Kris, my niece, with whom I have enjoyed good Christian fellowship.

They all profess to be believers in Christ, so I hope to see them in heaven. I recently enjoyed worshipping with my youngest nephew, Paul, and his family in their Harvest Bible Chapel, under the good preaching of Pastor James McDonald. Bill and Joan have both passed on to heaven, I trust, as I talked to each of them before they died.

After retirement, Bill wrote some short stories about his life. They remind me of O. Henry's short stories, so I would like to share just a couple of them with you.

Before we begin, I must explain something to you. When I was five years old, we used to go, sometimes, to the White Castle Restaurant. They sold little hamburgers for five cents, as I remember it. At the same time, we got the funny papers (comics). One of the popular comics of the time was *Popeye*, the strong sailorman, who had a big fat friend named Wimpy. I was a chubby little kid, at the time, and my father, looking at me, said, "There is Wimpy!" Some eighth-grade girls heard it and started calling me Wimpy. I got very angry and started chasing them. Anyway, the name stuck; that was my nickname all the way into my twenties.

CAPTAIN MIDNIGHT WINGS

Wimpy, my little brother was 8. I was 10. We lived on the southeast side in a 3 flat at 81st and Anthony. The building is no longer there. It's now under the Chicago Skyway.

Our backyard butted up against a raised railroad track. Passenger trains and freights rumbled past, night and day, unnoticed and unheard.

Two of our playmates were the Kelly boys who lived on the second floor. The Kellys didn't have a telephone. On the third floor lived Mr. and Mrs. Walsh. Mr. Walsh had a red face and white hair.

Back in those days, around supper time, kids listened to the radio. Their heroes were Jack Armstrong, "The All-American Boy," Orphan Annie, Captain Midnight and some others.

One evening, Capt. Midnight told us if we hurry to our local Skelly gas station, we could get real Captain Midnight wings free with a fill up of Skelly gasoline. Better move quickly as supplies are limited.

After school the next day, I told Bobby Kelly about the free wings offer. We were excited about the possibility. We didn't have a Skelly close to us. As a matter of fact, we didn't have a car—and neither did the Kellys.

But I thought I knew of a Skelly Oil way down about 89th and South Chicago Avenue. That was a long way from 81st and Anthony—and it was in a Polish neighborhood. We weren't Polish.

Polish went to Bowen High School. They always had good teams because their players were old guys. When those kids got to be 13 or 14, they'd quit school and work a few years in the steel mills. When they were 17 or 18 they'd go back to high school as freshmen. Grownups playing against kids!

Well, anyway, I got Wimpy and the Kelly boys and we decided to find the Skelly station-and hopefully get our Captain Midnight wings.

Eight long blocks later, tired, but anxious, we saw the gas station. The gas guy said, "yes, I still have some wings left."

It was a bright copper set of wings pinned on a card to write your name on as a club member.

I told him that we didn't own an automobile—but if we did, we'd use Skelly all the time. The guy laughed and then gave us each a pair of Captain Midnight wings!

As we left the oil reeking gas station, it was starting to get dark. Tired, but happy, we began our trek home.

A block or so down South Chicago Avenue we had to walk past a group of Polish. They were all bigger than us. We held our breath. "What are you guys doing in our neighborhood?" demanded a cigarette smoking Polish.

"Nothin'", I said, squeezing the Captain Midnight wings in my pocket. The Kellys and Wimpy looked to me for direction.

"Ya wanna fight?" The smoker asked.

I didn't think it was a good idea. Not that I couldn't fight. Just a week before I beat up Robert Giest. Hugo, our janitor, gave me 25 cents to fight Robert—and I did—up till the time his mother came out to break it up.

But the Polish were big guys.

I told the Kelly's, "Let's go," and started pushing past. After a few nervous steps, I noticed that Wimpy wasn't with us.

Looking back, there he was, swinging away at the biggest Polish. Wimpy was a pretty darn good fighter—until he got into high school and found Jesus—Then he switched to wrestling.

Back I ran and grabbed his arms and pulled him away from the Polish. "No, no, no," he cried. I yelled, "We're going home!"

Arriving home just before suppertime, we proudly showed Mom our treasures—shiny copper Captain Midnight wings.

I told Mom, "Look, we can pin them on our jackets or shirts." Mom said, "They are very nice. Now, go and wash your hands, it's almost time for Dad and dinner."

Soon the front door opened and in came Dad from work—and a long ride on the street car.

He smiled and said, "Hello, boys—what have you been doing today?"

AUNT "REE" AND THE LETTUCE CIGARETTES

The year was 1935 and my Aunt "Ree" was 70 years before her time.

She was a modern-day woman. She smoked lettuce leaves, drunk alcohol, colored her hair, had a child and was divorced before she was 25 years old.

We called her Aunt "Ree" because my oldest cousin couldn't say her full name—Hannah Marie. So, us kids simply said "Aunt Ree".

Hannah Marie was kind of skinny and always wore ankle length dresses—which I was sure covered her bow legs. Her red hair complemented her dark brown eyes. Large dangling earrings adorned her ears, while gaudy necklaces were usually draped around her neck

Oh Yes, bracelets, large plastic circles of all colors clanked from her wrists.

Aunt "Ree's son had moved to California, so she had me for company on the weekends. I was eight years old and she acted like I was her little boy. We both had red hair and brown eyes.

Aunt "Ree" lived on the far south side of Chicago, in a three flat in Roseland. She and her second husband—James Edward Walsh—

were members of the local Proto Athletic Club. I always thought his initials were kind of funny.

I don't know what was athletic about it. Because all they did was smoke, play cards, and drink beer.

Uncle Jim was a large, bulky Irishman, with a red face and wavy hair. He was a brick layer foreman and was out of town a lot. He worked with rough men, so he carried a black jack and brass knuckles, but he could magically pull Hershey bars out of his hair by saying, "Allah, Allah, Allah." I was impressed.

On Saturday, we were on Auntie's back porch and nosey Mrs. Napoli was coming down from the third floor. Aunt "Ree," who was smoking a cigarette, quickly handed it to me, saying, "Here, hold this, Billy. Mrs. Napoli doesn't know I smoke."

I took the cigarette and said, "Can I puff on it?" "Sure," said Auntie. As Mrs. Napolli walked past, staring at me, I took a puff, and of course, started coughing. Mrs. Napolli shook her head and said, "Tsk."

I asked Aunt "Ree" if I smoked a Lucky Strike? "No," she said, "It's a lettuce cigarette." "Oh?" I said, not knowing what else to say.

Back in the apartment, my Aunt's rooms were filled with interesting and exciting things. She had a great big pink sea shell, that held the roar of the ocean, if you put it up to your ear.

She had pillows with paintings on them— Niagara Falls, The World's Fair, and the Golden Gate Bridge. Aunt "Ree" had been all over the world!

Her house had a special smell about it. I'd say it was a mixture of smoke, beer and perfume.

Crime magazines were a favorite of Auntie's. I liked to look at them, too. Lots of pictures of dead guys and cops holding "tommy guns," with blood splashed all over.

This morning as Auntie was drinking her wake-up orange juice with "just a drop of vodka," she started to paint her toe nails with a bright red polish. She pulled up her long skirt. To my surprise, she didn't have bow legs, at all. Well, what do you know! But, they were pretty skinny. Then, why did she wear such long dresses?

We spent the afternoon at the Proto Club. Mostly, I was running errands, like getting cold beer from the corner tavern. Sometimes, I could even drink a little, between ginger ales, that is. Auntie said, "Just a couple of sips, Billy!"

That night I fell out of the bed and didn't even know it. My aunt woke me up and helped me back to bed. "Let's just keep this our little secret, Billy. I'll buy you a fudgesicle, before we take the streetcar back to your house," Auntie said.

1970 was the last time I heard from my Aunt. She called from California and said she just bought a new house. It was solid mahogany and just fit on a lot that was only 8 feet by 4 feet.

That's my Aunt "Ree." I still smile as I think of her. And I keep wondering about those lettuce cigarettes. (6/17/05 WCL)

***

This has been just a sample of my brother's writing. He wrote several more similar short stories but reading this one again reminded of me of "Aunt Ree." When they were kids, she and my uncle Willie were said to have gotten in trouble with my grandmother, when they sawed up a broom to make checkers to play on a linoleum floor, which had a square design, which they used for a "checkerboard."

Another story told about her was that she had a "tea room" in Prohibition days in which she served something other than tea. Nevertheless, she was very good to us. In fact, I remember, she would send us a letter or a note and, instead of signing her name, would draw a comical picture of a lady carrying a big bag because she always brought some "goodies" for us, whether candy or something else she bought for us.

CHAPTER 2

CHILDHOOD

I have just one memory which stands out in my mind when we lived somewhere around Roseland. It was a birthday party for a little girl named Frances Jean. She had long red, curly hair and was all dressed up in a beautiful dress; and it was, I think, her fifth birthday. I was only about four years old. Anyway, for some reason, she kissed me. There seemed to be several ladies there, and they all laughed loudly. I didn't know why she kissed me, or why everybody laughed. Nobody but my mother had ever kissed me, and I thought that was a bad thing to do—that is why everyone laughed. (Maybe that is why I was shy with girls in later life, except that I chased the big girls who called me Wimpy.)

The first school I remember attending was Avalon Park Elementary. My aunt Hilma was a teacher there. Bill was in her class, and I was, also, maybe around third grade. I have a vague memory of walking on top of some desks, maybe in first grade, and having to wear a dunce cap in a corner for doing so. The school was, I think, between 82nd and 83rd streets and near Stony Island on Chicago's south side. I remember getting haircuts at the Sears store for fifteen or twenty-five cents.

I remember walking home from school when a big kid knocked me down and held my hands on the icy sidewalk until it was said that my hands were frozen. When I got home, my mother poured cool, not hot water, on my hands, until they were restored. Thank God!

***

When we got a little older, we loved to go to the Avalon Theater, a huge and beautiful movie theater with lavish oriental ornamentation, which later become the church of a well-known evangelist, Robert Schambach.

Mom would give each of us eleven cents, a dime, for the show and one cent for candy. A year or two later, we got a nickel for candy, and we thought we were very rich. We saw movies like *Captain Blood*, with Errol Flynn; *Billy, the Kid*, and *Robin Hood*. Then we would go home and pretend that we were those characters.

On Good Friday, they had a preacher preaching the Gospel, in addition to the regular shows.

There was a railroad track on raised ground, right behind our apartment. In the winter, when it snowed, we loved to slide down that ground on our sleds. Some bad kids dug the ground out right under the tracks, trying to make the trains crash, I guess. But it never happened, thank God!

Another memory was running across Anthony Avenue, trying to beat a car. I didn't win and woke up on the other side of the street. I remember hearing my mother say, "He will be all right" when the driver of the car offered to take me to a hospital. God was already taking care of me! Also, I must have been about four years old when I told my mother I saw God in the clouds of the sky! She must not have seen what I saw, as she was not enthused!

We often had hoboes or tramps, we called them, who got off the freight trains and came to our back door, asking for food. Mother would give them food but did not let them come inside to eat. In those days, they did not have modern washing machines like today. They had the kind you run by hand, with "wringers." Monday was always "Wash Day." Mom would hang the clothes on clotheslines in the summer. One Monday, I don't remember if we went out somewhere, after she hung a whole yard full of clothes, but when she went out to check our clothes, there were no clothes on the lines. She called the police, who asked her to estimate the cost of the missing clothes. She said it may have been worth a hundred dollars, knowing that was a lot of money in those days! Of course, we never saw the clothes again. But we figured it must have been one of the hoboes from the freight trains who was bold enough to take the clothes in broad daylight.

There was a huge vacant lot that stretched about two blocks toward Stony Island Avenue, which we called the Big Prairie. We loved to set fires there but could never get a good one going. (Thank God!) I don't know where we got the matches. Must have taken them from home. We also used to catch garter snakes and put them in a glass jar.

As far as athletics, I considered it quite an accomplishment when I learned to throw "a spiral" with a football at nine years of age. But before that, I remember, I cried once when I couldn't field a ground ball, playing softball. That same year, we moved to an apartment, about three miles farther west, 82nd and Marshfield Avenue.

I suppose I was thought of as a pretty good boy, growing up, but I was a *sinner*, like everyone else! We kids of ten, eleven, twelve years of age thought it was our right to go out and raise hell on Halloween. It was a time to dump people's cans of ashes (from their coal fires) on their porches. I was no kind of a leader, but I seemed to take the lead in this deviltry. I would find some rocks and put out a streetlight or two. Looking back, I don't know why I did it because I do *not* remember being rebellious to my own parents…except once when Robert Kelly, my pal who lived upstairs, and I set fire to our coal bin. I don't know what happened. Someone must have found out and put the fire out! It seemed, in one season in our lives, we wanted to be arsonists. I believe we were ten years old and thought we were real *cool*—although that term was not used, as such, for years to come. Another bad thing I remember doing was stealing fruit from a store around 82nd and Ashland and taking grapes from a yard, farther south. Then once,

I sneaked into the Highland Theater at 79th and Ashland. There was someone else with me when I did these things. I believe I was trying to show how bad I was, or as in the Theater, I went along with my older companion, who was used to sneaking in. But that didn't excuse me.

So you can see, I was a sinner, like every other human on this earth! I had been baptized and was very serious about it. I remember, we had a rather large group from our Sunday school who had made decisions on "Decision Sunday" to be baptized. We were given robes to wear for the baptism, and the boys were baptized first. When we went to change our clothes, I heard one of the boys, maybe thirteen years old, say, "Come on, let's hurry back to see the girls get out of the water." Even at that age, I knew what he meant. Lustfully, he wanted to see the girls' bodies exposed by the clinging wet garments as they got out of the water. I knew that was wrong! But that was not the problem I had that day. My problem was that I fought with my brother that day, and I knew that there was no change in my life. I thought that I understood what baptism meant and what coming to a decision meant. But I didn't realize, until four years later, that I had never *repented of my sins*!

There was one incident I remember while attending the Cook School on the south side of Chicago. During the morning outside recess, the local bully—a big boy, about five feet, eleven inches tall—would not let me and two of our classmates back in school, when the bell rang and recess was over. We were afraid of the bully; thus, we were more than thirty minutes late getting back to class. We were fifth-graders, as I recall, and were not punished for the incident, so perhaps, the bully was.

I should say something more about fifth to eighth grades. At Cook Elementary School, I remember we had to crouch or kneel against the hallway walls to practice for possible air raids, as it was World War II then. (Years later, as a sub teacher, I would help children, in the same way, but for Tornado Drills.) Bill and I also started a new church, Foster Park Baptist, going only to Sunday school at first. John (Jack) Perry and his brother Jim also attended. Jim was in Bill's class in school, and they became good friends, later travelling together in Europe. Jack was also a friend in my class. By the time we graduated from Calumet High School, Jack had the highest rating—cadet major in the Reserve Officers Training Corps.

I believe it was in fifth or sixth grade that I met Randall (Randy) McNally, when we shared a desk together for a music class. Randy and his family were strict Roman Catholics, but we became good friends. He and his sisters, Elaine and Rojean, were champion caliber baton twirlers, and they performed with marching bands.

Just before eighth grade, we moved to 85th and Wood Street. Foster Park School was right across the street. It was a small, rather new school, about ¾ of a mile from Cook School; but Randy lived just a block away, at 84th and Wood. Randy had been going to Cook and would continue to do so, probably because it was a bigger and older school. And of course, he wanted me to continue at Cook and walk to school with him. I worried about it all summer but finally decided it was too easy to go across the street. I would not be going back to Cook.

Nevertheless, we were still friends. One of the things we did in the neighborhood, in which Randy participated, was to have mile races, running three times around the school on the sidewalks. Later, Randy went to Mt. Carmel (Catholic) High School, then on to Notre Dame, where he was on the Track or cross-country team. Still later, he attended Washington University in St. Louis and became a plastic surgeon. Some of the Chicago Blackhawks became his patients.

Starting Calumet High School, there was a myth going around that they would be playing all kinds of tricks on us "Freshies." My good friend, down the block, Vernon Olson told his parents not to expect him to come home with his pants on. They called it being "pantsed," but I never saw it happen to anyone. And I never worried about it. They also talked about seniors trying to sell you a steam-heated locker, but it was all hype, trying to get us freshmen nervous.

In those high school days, during summer, we played what we called Fast Pitching with a rubber ball thrown against a school wall, where we had outlined the strike zone. We kept track of the count and played regular ball games. Bill; Carl Boehme, down the block; and Eugene "Yoot" Paine were fastball pitchers. Vernon and I were not so fast, so we tried to throw "curves." I think we all threw our arms "out," trying to throw that lightweight ball. Billy Mulligan, from down at 83rd street, would play with us sometimes. He liked to dramatize the game as he went along, as if it were the Cubs playing the Yankees, or someone. Billy was a pretty good young boxer. He went to St. Ignatius High School. I believe he became a coach, himself, as did "Bud" Heyne, whose father was a basketball coach—and he followed in his footsteps at Western Kentucky.

The Arneberg family lived on our block. There were three of the boys who played football for St. Leo High School, not far from us. Jimmy was maybe a year older than Bill, and we loved him. A real nice young man. Every year in Chicago, the City bowl was held, with the champions of the Catholic and the Public League, playing football for the City Championship. Jimmy's older brother, John, played defensive end for Leo, who were the Catholic champions. Billy DeCorrevont was the Tilden Tech quarterback, who later played for the Chicago Cardinals but didn't last long. Arneberg was a lineman. As I was told, to start the game, De Correvont went back twice to pass. But each time, John ran through the defense to tackle DeCorrevont for big losses.

We used to play touch football in the cement alley, and I would throw the passes. Because of my heart murmur, I was not supposed to run. Well, Bobby Smith used to play with us, although he was about three years younger than me. Later, he went on to play football at Leo, and later, at Notre Dame. Well, I won't mention any names, but someone came to me twice and offered me money, if I would beat up Bobby Smith, and then, Billy Mulligan. But I refused, as both were friends of mine. I had nothing against them. Anyway, Bobby was too young for me, although he was big for his age. And Billy was a boxer. I doubt if I could take him, anyway. Strangely, about that time, Bobby Breen, Smith's stepbrother, who was my age, tried to pick a fight with me. I had no doubt I could take him, but he was my friend. I had no reason to fight him, so I just shrugged him off.

CHANGING NEIGHBORHOOD

It was the first day of school, September 1945. I was starting my Junior year at Calumet High School, 81st and May St,. but was unaware that the neighborhood had been changing. I saw some students marching or demonstrating on Racine Avenue, as I came to school. I didn't know what it was about, but I knew some of them. And being in a playful mood, I thought I would join them. It would be a way to get out of having to go to school. I soon learned what it was about. They were protesting that a handful of Negro students were entering our school for the first time.

I did not go to school that day but, later, repented because I had nothing against anyone. I had just gotten caught up with the mob. There were a few students still protesting and trying to block the entrance into the school the next morning, but I walked right in. In the hallway I saw a black girl, waiting to register. Someone yelled out, "Nigger lover!" I don't know if they meant me, but it made no difference to me. Anyone in the neighborhood had a right to attend our school.

But I heard the girl say, "You may love me, but I don't love you." Again, I don't know if she was trying to talk to me, but she soon would be in my English class, where I had no dealings with her, good or bad. There was no more racial strife after that, as far as I know. The only other black student who was in my class was Mel Chenier, who was in my swimming class, as Calumet had a swimming pool. Mel became a halfback (as they were called at that time—i.e., a running back) on the football team. He was short, but fast, and got along fine, as far as I knew.

CHAPTER 3

CONVERSION AND CALL TO MINISTRY

Going back a few years, to the summer after my sophomore year in high school, I had recovered from the ringworm infection and had gotten a job as a soda jerker at the local K&K Drug store and was paid thirty-five cents an hour. Bill and another of our neighborhood friends had worked there before. I was "sitting pretty," I thought. They had told me I could eat all the ice cream I wanted. But neither Mr. King, the owner, nor Doc Marvel, his druggist, had told me that. Nevertheless, when it was not busy, toward the end of the night, I would make myself a milkshake with about eight dips of ice cream! Not only that, but I would take a pack of cigarettes home without paying for them, any time I felt like it. I knew smoking was not good for me, especially as I had athletic aspirations. But I decided ahead that I would only smoke for a month or so, which is what I did. It was my little bit of rebellion. Even as I write, I now realize I should have confessed to Mr. King and paid for what I took. It is many years too late to do so now. Mr. King and Marvel have probably died, decades ago.

But I began to have digestive problems, or so I thought. Some said it was a nervous stomach. But I know now, it was nothing less than conviction of sin. My father had told me, "The whiter the bread, the sooner you are dead." So I became very particular about my diet and would eat only whole wheat bread, and I drank *no* soda pop.

At the beginning of the year, our pastor in the Baptist church, where we attended, suggested that we all should read the Bible all the way through, beginning with Genesis, so I began. When I got to the book of Ecclesiastes, God began speaking to me. I read, *"Vanity of vanities, saith the preacher, vanity of vanities, all is vanity"* (Eccles. 1:2, KJV).

I found that vanity means selfishness and emptiness. I looked at the lives of the football players I so admired. (Calumet High School had won the South Section Championship, defeating Fenger High, 6–0, for the first time in years.) But I saw in their lives, and in my own, nothing but *selfishness and emptiness.* I read further in the book of Isaiah 1:18 (KJV), *"Come now and let us reason together, though your sins be as scarlet, they shall be as white as snow, though they be red like crimson, they shall be as wool."*

I had been baptized at twelve years of age. I had been sincere but had never really repented for my sins. I was still *lost.* I don't remember the date, but it was in the month of May 1946. I must have weighed about one hundred pounds. All my athletic dreams were gone. I knew I was a lost sinner and needed to be saved. One day, in the lunch room of Calumet High School, with perhaps hundreds of teenagers around me, I bowed my head and prayed to the Lord, saying, "This is the world, Lord. I give up the world for you." Later, on my way home from school (I was so weak, I had to stop and rest on a park bench in Foster Park on my way home from school) I bowed my head, again and prayed, "Lord Jesus, come into my heart, and be my Savior, and forgive all my sins." I don't remember praying anything else, but He did come in. And I was saved.

I began picking up papers and trash when I saw them. Because this was "my Father's world," as the song says. Everything began to change for me, as a poem says, the "grass looked greener, the sky bluer," etc.

I was seldom late for school. We almost always walked the mile or so it took, in about twenty minutes of fast walking. But one day, I was late. On the form for tardiness, for the reason for tardiness, I wrote, "I refused to hurry," which I attributed to the new change in my life. I read 2 Corinthians 5:17, "*If any man be in Christ, he is a new creature, old things are passed away, behold, all things are become new.*" Later, the change in life caused me to do the opposite, to hurry *not* to be late.

As I was about to enter my senior year in high school, my parents must have worried about my loss of weight and change of habits. Since I was "born again," "the Word of God" became my guide. I spent hours in my room, reading the Bible and meditating. They took me to the doctor, who weighed me and found I weighed only 90 pounds. They put me in the hospital and diagnosed my case, as I remember it, as an underactive thyroid gland and malnutrition. I have been told by some it must have been an overactive gland that caused me to lose weight. That might sound plausible, but I was not an energetic, nervous person, which someone might think would go with an overactive gland.

They put me in bed for some time and started serving me big meals. One hour after the meals, they would serve me about a glass and a half of a drink called Meekin's Mix. It was made with powdered milk, two eggs, flavored with chocolate and vanilla, and I loved it. But the damage had already been done. I was underweight and gained very slowly. Also, about that time, they found that I had a heart murmur, and I could not take gym for the rest of that semester. The heart murmur, they said, may have been a result of the scarlet fever I had at four years of age. Mother had gotten the fever first and gone to the hospital, and Bill and I had been infected. But Bill had a milder case.

ASSURANCE OF SALVATION

I believe it was because no one led me to the Lord, I just prayed for myself, that I began to have doubts about my salvation. It was not a constant thing. But periodically, it would come upon me. I would have terrible fears, and then, I would feel even worse because I doubted. It did not stop me from continuing to seek the Lord, however. Later, at Wheaton College, even though I loved to go to the daily chapel services, I still remember hearing a noted preacher in the Baptist Church there and talked to him after the service about my problem. He told me that the devil could take away my joy, but he couldn't take away my salvation.

This lack of full assurance of salvation bothered me at times for a total of seven years! Finally, I wrote about it to my good friend from Wheaton College, Dick Shrout. He wrote back, "What's a matter, can't you read?" and then quoted such verses as 1 John 5:9–13, particularly verses 11 and 12, *"This is the record, that God has given to us Eternal Life. He that has the Son, has life. And he that has not the Son of God, has not life." Thank God, I have never had a doubt since that day!* Salvation has nothing to do with our emotions; it is all about *believing* the Word of God! I had heard these things before, but now, it got to me! I can hardly believe I had doubts all those years! They were from no one but the devil. And truly, the devil is a liar! It is the same answer for those who think they have committed the unpardonable sin. If they had committed that sin, they would not be concerned about it because they would have said a definite no to God, concerning salvation through trusting in Christ.

That is why I can have perfect confidence that when I come to the end of my days on earth, I can have no fear, for I know where I am going. *Praise the Lord! "God hath not given us the Spirit of fear, but of power, and of love, and of a sound mind!"* (2 Tim. 1:7). And that is why I know that my beloved wife, Bettye, is with the Lord, despite any doubts she may have had. Why? Because I know that she had "the Son of God" in her life, and she trusted Him for her salvation.

MY CALLING

Meanwhile, things were happening in my spiritual life. I had offered myself as a Sunday school teacher at twenty years of age, when my Baptist church was asking for people to make such commitments. I felt I was no kind of a leader. I knew nothing about it, but "if you want me, here I am." I started to teach a junior-age class. I studied hard at it and did my best. I also took a Gra-Y club, a YMCA club in which I became a mentor for grade school boys. One of my young members had tried to commit suicide, so I felt this club, just like Sunday school, was a very serious position. But as I look back, I realize now, at that time, I did not even know that Jesus was God, although I had been born again, but I had not yet come to assurance of my salvation. I had prayed for myself in that high school lunchroom, and on my way home, in the park, but no one "led me to the Lord." It was all my own subjective thoughts. I had talked to no one, no pastor, nor youth worker, yet I knew something happened between God and me. But I was also assailed by doubts, whether I was REALLY SAVED. Later I learned it was just temptations from the Devil. Now I can hardly believe that I doubted. And I did not yet know that the Holy Spirit was a Person! I thought He was just some kind of feeling.

But God was dealing with me. I knew that there was something beyond flesh and blood going on in my teaching, and I began listening to radio programs from the Moody Bible Institute, which helped a lot because I was not yet grounded in the Word. A few months before this, I was in the hospital with swollen glands in the neck. (Maybe it was related to the thyroid problem I had earlier.) One of my aunts, Matilda (or Tillie), gave me a book written by the track star, Gil Dodds, holder of the World Indoor mile record at that time—4.06 minutes. (He was later to be my gym teacher at Wheaton College.) In the book, he mentioned someone who was called to be a missionary, or at least, made that decision. This bothered me a great deal. God didn't want me to be a missionary, did He? At least, I hoped not.

About this time, a missionary to India, named Dr. Blanchard, came to our Baptist Church. He put on a skit, showing how he tried to persuade Hindus to come to Christ and be converted and how it affected him when they did not accept his words. He was very sad because he knew that accepting Jesus as their Savior was the only way their sins could be forgiven. I was very touched by his words and was almost ready to take the next boat to India! But after a while, my zeal cooled off.

Finally, one night, I could not sleep. I tossed and turned and knew I had to decide, one way or another. I finally said yes to God, that I would be a missionary. I could not sleep until I had made that commitment to God. I made it known in the church that I had made that decision. What I didn't know was that I would not set foot on foreign soil as a missionary, until some forty years later. But it was still a momentous experience for me. I meant it with all my heart. I knew I had given myself to God, and my life would never be the same after that. I belonged to God. Looking back, from hindsight, I would say that what happened that night was that I had dedicated my life to God for fulltime Christian service.

I got in touch with the American Baptist Foreign Mission Society, to see what was to be my next step. I found that a BA or BS degree was required first, and then a BD degree (Bachelor of Divinity, requiring a three-year seminary course). I was advised to get my first degree at a Baptist College in southern Illinois. Our Baptist denomination was somewhat liberal, and when I saw the information from the Baptist College, it illustrated dances that were sponsored at the school. I was not impressed. I was not going to school for social reasons. Was this the school for me? The other alternative seemed to be Wheaton College, just west of Chicago, which was considered a fundamental or conservative school. Was I ready for that?

CHAPTER 4

LIFE AFTER CONVERSION

WEIGHTLIFTING

From working at the K&K Drugstore, both Bill and I became interested in a magazine called *Strength and Health*. The editor and founder's name was Bob Hoffman, who became an authority on weightlifting, and later became an Olympic coach. They showed pictures and stories about muscular men. They were members of the York Barbell Club at York, Pennsylvania. The magazine stories told us that the way to build big muscles and super health was through progressive weight training. We were enthused. The years were 1945 and 1946. This was before any schools or athletic teams used weight training for their athletes, although I understand Hoffman started the York Barbell Company as early as 1932, so it did take some years before it became famous. The reason was, probably, in addition to weightlifting being a rather new idea, there was a big myth going around that it would make you *muscle-bound*. Of course, today we know there is no truth to that rumor, as today, all the successful schools and professional teams use weights (such as barbells, dumbbells, etc.).

To illustrate the philosophy of the power of progressive exercise with weights, the story was told of a young man, probably in Italy, named Milo, who carried his baby calf to town every day. This went on for some months, as the calf was growing into a young cow. Milo did not notice the gradual increase in the weight of the calf he carried because his muscles were growing stronger every day, enabling him to carry the now enlarged animal. This shows the principle of the body increasing in strength to compensate for the increase in resistance. Hoffman tells how, as a youngster, he watched the sailors on Lake Erie. He wondered why they were so strong, until he noticed how hard they would work as they prepared to sail away. Then, they would rest. From this observation came the overload or irregular method of training, meaning heavy training one day and resting the next day, not *daily* exercising.

We thought we had discovered a great secret! The only thing for me was, although newly converted and having always been interested in exercise and sports, I now weighed only ninety pounds, recovering from malnutrition and an underactive thyroid gland, as the doctor stated. It was also discovered that I had a "heart murmur," which means there is some leakage when the heart is pumping the blood throughout the body, causing the organ to work harder to compensate for the leakage. Therefore, I started my senior year in high school, unable to take gym. I still played touch football after school, except now, I was the passer and not the receiver, as I was not supposed to run. Just two years before, in gym tests, if my memory is correct, I did 125 consecutive sit-ups, resulting in sore abdominal muscles for the next two months and 80 squat-jumps, which was an exercise I did for the first time. As I recall, we only had two or two and one-half minutes to do the exercises. Looking back, now in my old age, I can hardly believe I did them that fast.

I don't remember where I got the money, probably from my parents, but I sent $20.00 to York, Pennsylvania, and received a one hundred-pound York barbell with illustrations of ten exercises I could do. At first, even the fifteen-pound bar was too heavy, so I began doing the exercises with a broomstick! I had asked the doctor if I could exercise, and he said, "Yes, but don't walk too far." Apparently, he was saying the only kind of exercise I could do was *walking*. But *Strength and Health* magazine talked about the "iron pills," meaning weight training, and that during the war, they had found that wounded soldiers recovered more quickly when they exercised.

So for the next year or so, we exercised regularly, Bill and I, also bringing our neighborhood buddies down to our basement where we worked out. I remember some of them saying they worked out so hard that they could hardly climb the stairs to go home. I seem to remember using seventy pounds in the arm curl exercise, which I can hardly do now in my old age!

In the summer though, we loved to play baseball. If someone asked me what I wanted to be "when I grew up," I would say without hesitation, "A baseball player." I think it must have been my junior year in high school before I lost so much weight, when a dark cloud came over me, so to speak. Someone said, "Just think, pretty soon we are going to be too old to play baseball like this, every day." Wow! I never thought about that! But it was true. I had to admit it. Of course, I was never going to be a baseball player. I wasn't that good. I was just a skinny kid, who thought he could run fast and hit hard liners and ground balls. But that is what we young white boys thought. We could be anything we wanted to be "when we grew up." I didn't think about it then, but I wonder how the "colored boys" whom I had seen on my way downtown on the "El" felt about their future?

I should mention another ordeal I went through. I was about fourteen years old, on a summer evening, about nine o'clock, when my neighbor, Carl, brought home a brand-new bicycle. We were all thrilled to see it. Carl and his father, and Bill and I, and maybe some other neighbor, were there. I asked Carl if I could try his new bicycle. So I rode it down the block, made a U-turn and drove it back and made another U-turn, at the same time, bringing the vehicle to a stop, so I could get off. But something happened. I lost my balance and started to fall. I did not want anything to happen to Carl's new bike, so I made sure that the bike fell on me so it wouldn't hit the ground. So I put out my left arm to break the fall. Right away, I knew something was wrong. My arm began to hurt at the elbow. But my main concern was that nothing should happen to the bicycle.

The next morning, my arm was still hurting and swollen at the elbow. My parents decided to take me to a doctor. The doctor was very happily preparing to leave for a vacation. He said it was just a sprain in the elbow. He bound my arm up and put it in a sling, and said I should take the sling off once a day, move it around a little, and he would see me in two weeks. But when I took the sling off, my arm seemed very heavy. I couldn't hold it up. By the end of the two weeks, there seemed to be a big knob on my elbow, and I couldn't bend it.

We never went back to that doctor but went to an osteopath, which, in those days, was like the chiropractors of today. He was an old man who was a friend of the family. Thus, began my ordeal. Every Saturday, I had to take a bus ride to the southeast side of Chicago, and the osteopath would work on my arm, twisting and rotating it around. We would hear "snap, snap, pop." False tissue breaking, he said. He also told me, at home, I should lie on the floor on top of my outstretched arm, and try to push it straight. Also, I was to double my arm up, the best way I could, and push it at the shoulder, against a door or wall. In addition to all this, I was to carry a can of paint, with my palm facing out, as much as I could, walking back and forth through the house, for ten minutes at a time.

I would keep track of how many times a day I did it. Strange though it seems now, I was still afraid of the dark, but walked through some dark rooms, as I did it after school and at night. Looking back, I never thought of turning on the lights, I guess that was my parent's thing, in those days. Every Saturday, I had an upset stomach as I traveled to see the osteopath, knowing that what he was going to do to me would hurt. But I never complained or told anyone about it. I considered this part of my character as coming from my Swedish forbears, who were considered able to suffer in silence.

But, when I got to my osteopathic doctor, he was displeased that I had not held the gains made from the last visit, when he claimed to have broken down the "false tissue." Despite all this, I was still interested in osteopathic theory, which states that the human body has within it, all that is needed to fight disease, when the body is put in structural integrity. Several years later, I visited the Osteopathic College, and they considered me as a student, even though I did not yet have the required bachelor's degree.

However, about this time, my parents came to my rescue. We all agreed that my arm was not getting any better. So it was decided I should go to an MD (medical doctor). It was now wartime. (WWII). I don't know how my parents got in contact with Dr. Magnuson, who was the head of the Veterans Administration Medical Department. He apparently told my parents that surgery was necessary to remove the head of the radius bone and to transplant a ligament. What had happened was that it was originally a broken bone in the elbow (head of the radius) and calcium material, which was supposed to heal the break, had leaked out and formed the knob on my elbow, while it was in the sling.

My parents apparently told Dr. Magnuson they could not afford the amount he told them it would cost, so he asked them how much they could pay, and they agreed on a price, which I'm sure was nothing like prices today. (Apparently, they did not have health insurance in those days.) I woke up from the surgery, dreaming that my friend Carl was hitting my elbow with a stick, which was strange because I certainly never blamed Carl, who, incidentally, is a Christian, and one of my few old friends, still in our late eighties.

But I am so thankful to God that I have been able to use my left arm for my whole life! It is not as strong as my right arm, and I have had some difficulties with it in weightlifting exercises, but *"My grace is sufficient for thee, for my strength is made perfect in weakness. Most gladly, therefore will I rather glory in my infirmities, that the power of Christ may rest upon me"* (2 Cor. 12:9, KJV).

ARMY DAYS

About that time, after I had been graduated from high school and had finished one year at Wilson Junior College, my brother, Bill, told me of a new program whereby I could join the Army and only had to serve one year in active service. Otherwise, if I was drafted, I would have to serve at least two years. They called it Universal Military Training, the Selective Service Act of 1948. You had to be eighteen years of age, so I signed up about a month before my nineteenth birthday. I was shipped to Fort Riley, Kansas, and from there, on to Fort Sill, Oklahoma.

I had gained a little weight by this time but also had grown a couple of inches, so I was quite thin at about 120 pounds. I was in the 6th Armored Field Artillery Battalion with other eighteen-year-olds, mostly from the state of Illinois. I remember only one other from Chicago, a kind of wild little guy, and one (from a different battalion) from New York, most of them being from downstate Illinois. Judging from how they talked, they all seemed like southerners to me, although some were from Ottawa, Lasalle-Peru, and Rock Island, in the northern part of the state.

First, we had basic or "boot training." It was six weeks long, if I remember rightly. The colonel, or whoever was the man in charge of us, said, "Good morning, gentlemen, this is the Sixth Armored Field Artillery Battalion." And as he was standing in front of what we would call a tank, with a piece of artillery pointing out of it, he said, "And this is a 105 millimeter Howitzer." This is what we were going to deal with from then on. We started the day with "Drill Call." That is, we all had to hurry and line up, and they would call your name, to make sure we were all there.

Of course, before that, about six a.m., while it was still dark out, someone would play the bugle, singing, "I can't get 'em up, I can't get 'em up, I can't get 'em up in the morning! Captain's worst of all." Then the sergeant would storm in, yelling, "Hurry up! Hurry up! Clean up this [deleted] house!" I was always slow at it. There was not that much to do. All you had to do was make sure your bed was made, your foot locker in order, and a little sweeping.

There were some well-built guys, and a couple of them were married already, although all of us had to be signed up before our nineteenth birthday. Some of them looked to me like they were about twenty-five, and one guy looked like he had receding hair, like he was already going bald! Some of these guys were made acting corporals or something, and one of them said to me, "Lythberg, there is a certain amount of work the platoon has to do." That is all he said and walked away. So I didn't pay any attention to him because I was already sweeping the floor.

We always had to "hurry up and wait" in the Army. When we were through cleaning up, we had to hurry up and line up at the mess hall. Then we had to wait there until they opened the door. After breakfast, we had exercises. One day, I did something wrong, I guess, because the lieutenant told me I would lead the exercise the next day and gave me a paper illustrating the exercise I was to lead. So I studied it and practiced it, but he *never* called on me to do it. And I *never* asked him about it.

Our officers sometimes gave us demerits. (I forget what lapses or misdemeanors they were for.) But I do remember I was given one or two of them, and I had to mow the captain's lawn. I was a little slow about it, so the sergeant told me I should have eaten more eggs that morning.

One of the hardest thing we had to do, I think, was a sixteen-mile hike, carrying full equipment and our M-1 rifles. Some of the guys were falling out toward the end, and I sure felt like it, but I kept going. Finally, we made it, and we could stop and rest and eat the rations we carried with us!

Another event that was difficult for me was bivouac—camping out and sleeping in tents. What made it hard was that it was in the winter, and it just happened to snow, which was very rare in Oklahoma. They tried to give me hot coffee to warm me up, but I couldn't drink it, although my family drank coffee. I just never liked it. It was the same with liquor. I tried wine and beer. I didn't really like the taste of it. (And wouldn't drink it, if I did like it, as I knew it was not good for me.) In the summer, we had bivouac again. But that was a breeze. We also picked out places where we would dig foxholes. But we didn't dig them, just outlined where they would have been.

Another scary thing was crawling through, what were told, was live machine gun fire. We had to crawl close to the ground. Other times, we had to run as fast as we could. As if we were escaping live fire. At one point, I sprained my ankle, and it was swollen and sore. I went to the medics to see if I could stay off my feet for a while but was told, "No, tighten your boot, as tight as you can get it, and go on as usual. That is the best thing for a sprained ankle." I followed their advice and eventually, the swelling went down, and it was healed.

After basic training, we were given a lot of films, day after day, about the different aspects of the Armored Field Artillery: the gun crew, who loaded and fired the artillery; the forward observers who, like spies, went ahead to find the enemy and called back specifics, so we could fire the guns on them; the radio-telephone operators; and the fire direction control. They gave us tests, which were supposed to show our approximate IQs (intelligence quotient—my score came out as 129, which was fairly high. But I was never a brilliant student). I was the type that had to work hard for my grades and was never anywhere near the top of the class, even in high school.

They offered me the opportunity to take the exam for admission to West Point. I believe it was Lieut. Jones who said I was recommended for *further military training.* The only thing about it was that I would have to stay in the Army for at least an additional three years, after graduation from West Point.

I didn't think too much about it because I was not interested in a military career. And of course, there was no assurance that I would pass the test for entrance to West Point. I entered the Army to give myself a chance to make up my mind what I was going to do for the rest of my life. I had been Born Again, but was not yet well grounded in the Lord and His Word. Because of my experience with an osteopath, I was considering that field, although I already believed that God can heal, Himself, without medicine. I was yet to have an experience with God, yielding myself to Him for fulltime service, but I did not know that, at the time.

I was placed in the FDC (fire direction control) unit, and we were given at least one week of films on that specialty, after a week of basic armored artillery films. But I couldn't grasp or understand what the films were all about until we actually began practicing what we had seen. There were only two or three of us in this specialized training. We were trained for the position of *computer*. I don't remember if the personal computers that most of us have today were yet introduced to the public, but they were about to be. However, this was a different kind of computing. From information that we received from the forward observer, basically, the distance to the target, we had tools that would tell us just how to aim the artillery and fire it.

One of my friends in FDC was given the job of computer. I was also trained and could do it, if necessary, but I was called the recorder and was also a radio-telephone operator. The forward observer had the "address" of Art 26 and ours was Art 21. Art 26 would call and say, "Art 21, this is Art 26, I have a fire mission!"

I would answer, "Art 26, this is Art 21, send your fire mission!"

Art 26 would answer, "Enemy infantry in the open, five thousand yards away." Then our computer would figure, with his tools, how high to raise the 105 mm. Howitzer artillery to reach the enemy five thousand yards away. I would record the figures he gave me and give them to the officer, and he would shout out, "Fuse quick [or Fuse delay] Elevation 256 [or whatever the computer had found]." Then he would say, "Fire when ready!" or "Fire at my command!" and I would write on my sheet, "Fire WR" or "Fire AMC."

We did not fire just once, but we did it by "bracketing." We did not try to hit the target, but tried to hit just beyond it. Maybe ten or twenty feet beyond. Then we would try to hit the same distance before the target. We would continue with this procedure, getting closer and closer, until we hit it.

We were called School Troops or Show Troops, and we would put on demonstrations for foreign observers who came to learn the military operations for their own countries. Lt. Jones was our officer-in-charge, and we got pretty friendly. He once said to me, "Lythberg, you are one of the few righteous men we have here." I thought that was quite a compliment. But one time, he got a little bit provoked by me. We were shooting from the top of a hill, and the foreign observers were down below, somewhere. I couldn't see them. But it was my job to yell out "SPLASH!" whenever our guns fired. One time I got to talking to the lieutenant and forgot to yell out, "SPLASH!" He was angry and let me know it. That was a big mistake! A lot of money was wasted in a shell being fired if they were not ready to see it. Thank God, it never happened again, and I heard no more about it from Lt. Jones.

Each armored tank had a crew who worked with the shells, which were rather large, and were passed quickly from one man to another, who slammed it into the artillery gun, while another of the crew fired it. (I don't remember exactly how they fired, as I only worked on the tank once.) But we, in FDC, were also part of the squad. Corporal Copenbarger—I think was the name of the leader of the squad. He was not one of us teenagers, but a little older, maybe in his thirties. He wanted to have a good squad, so he invited us over to his house for dinner one night. He did not stay in the barracks, but off the base in the nearby town, Lawton, Oklahoma.

Two guys on our squad played on our company baseball team, an Irish guy named Sullivan and an Italian, whose name I can't remember. They were both Roman Catholics. Suddenly, the corporal said, as if he couldn't believe it, "So you are all virgins?" They were embarrassed. I was not embarrassed but wondered why he would ask such a question. We didn't have any badge or sign on us, saying we were virgins, but we acknowledged that we were. Apparently, when we got passes and went to town on the weekends, some went looking for prostitutes. I went with a group one weekend, and they stopped in some plain building and talked with some plain appearing Indian young women. I had nothing to do with them and wanted nothing to do with them. We all left together. I don't know if any of them went back there later. If I knew that was what it was about, I wouldn't have gone with them in the first place.

The other little guy from Chicago bunked right next to me. One day, he asked if I would lend him some money, like five or ten dollars, I think it was, so I gave it to him. Later, I heard him talking to another fellow, apparently about some prostitutes they had. I don't know if he used my money for that or not, and I never asked him about it. But we got paid once a month, as I recall. I believe it was $150. Well, he got his money and laid it out on his bed. He made no motions toward me or said anything about repaying me for the loan, so I just politely picked up the amount he owed me from his bunk. He didn't like it at all and told me so. But I didn't care. That's the way I was in those days.

It was very hot when we had to get up early and go to the rifle range. We had only one day to practice, then we had to qualify with our M-1 rifles. I knew nothing about rifles or guns, had never gone hunting, or touched a rifle. But they told me just what to do. "Relax, get the target in your sites, and squeeze the trigger, slowly and gently, without moving anything else." The targets, I believe, were about one hundred yards away. There were guys out there, monitoring the targets. I think we got five points for a bull's-eye, in the center of the target, and decreasingly lower amounts for the other circles of the target. If you missed the target altogether, they waved a red flag, called Maggies' Drawers, and you got zero points. Thank God! I got the rating of *sharpshooter*. There was only one rating higher, that of "Expert."

Another experience was *guard duty*. It was so long ago that I can't remember the exact details. But it was at night, and I believe it was two hours on duty, and four hours off, so we could get some sleep. The off-duty room was not so nice, consisting of beds and dirty mattresses, as I recall. The total duration of the detail was twelve hours, divided among three recruits. So we each were on duty for a total of four hours. We had an area to patrol, walking back and forth, carrying our M-1 rifles, with us. After the guard duty, we would go on KP (kitchen police). But this first time, we were to take a prisoner to a jail or holding place. There were two of us with our M-1 rifles in the back of a truck, guarding him. Suddenly, the prisoner made a quick one-armed move and snatched the rifle right out of the other sleepy guard's hands! I had no time to think what I should do, thank God, for he immediately handed the rifle back to the guard, with a smirk on his face. Apparently, he just wanted to see if he could get away with it. I didn't tell anybody about it, and I don't think the other guard did either.

KP (kitchen police) was interesting. The head cook showed us how to wash dishes. That's right! They didn't have any dishwashing machines in those days. We were to put the silverware in the big dishpan first, then the large bowls, plates, and last, the glasses. Then he showed us how to break eggs, which I still do by that method today. You hit them sharply on the edge of the pan, with which you are cooking, and then you can divide the shells in two, as you let the egg matter fall nicely into the pan. The only other thing I remember doing on KP was to peel potatoes, which requires little comment.

MADE CORPORAL

In the spring of 1949, I was surprised to be given an official paper stating I had been made a corporal, which was grade four, after recruit, private, and private first class. However, I was not given any new uniforms with two stripes or any stripes to sew on, probably because our one-year service would soon be done, and we were to be transferred to reserve training for six years. But the training only lasted a few months, as I recall. We went to monthly meetings and were shown films on *laundry* work. But for the time being, I only remember one detail where I was called to work as a corporal. That was to lead the men in cleaning up a certain outside area. I don't think I did very well. I never had any thought or desire to be a leader. Later, I would learn that every Christian is to be a leader in some way, particularly those in the ministry.

I did not think of it, until now, but for that year in the Army, strangely, I do not recall seeing one *African American* among the recruits or any of the officers. I remember only one person who was not from Illinois. He was a young Jewish man from New York, whom I befriended, although he was called a communist by some of the others.

    Lastly, about the Army, let me say, I was called again to report back for full-time service in the Korean War, after being transferred to the Army reserve, but I requested and was granted a deferral because I was then attending college full time. But the next year, I was sent a letter telling me to report to California to an antiaircraft battalion. So I decided I would not ask for another deferral. However, it was not long before Congress passed a bill saying that reservists with prior duty would no longer be recalled for duty. My orders were revoked. I thank God, for I know it was Him, who kept me out of the Korean War. For war is hell, as Gen. Sherman said, in the Civil War days, confirmed by one of my friends who was *not* deferred for going to school. He said their forward observer relayed messages saying the target is "*the river of blood,*" apparently, of North Korean infantry.

CHAPTER 5

EDUCATION

I thank God for the education he has allowed me to have. But I must mention that no one should ever be *proud* or haughty about their education, neither should they look down critically on those who, for some reason, do not have the education that they have. In a coming chapter, we will consider our marriage, my beloved wife, Bettye and me. Her ambition in growing up was to become a college professor, which was never realized, but she did have some good education, particularly in becoming a graduate of Moody Bible Institute, in the days when they did not have so many black grads (1970). It was not long after our wedding when I realized, if not before, that she was indeed just as intelligent as I was (which may not be saying much). My assessment was that we were equal. She was not smarter than me, neither was I smarter than her. Some say that women are more emotional than men, that they seem to go by their feelings, rather than reason. But I learned, in our marriage, that it is often not emotion, but an unexplainable insight that women seem to have that men do not have. I say this because in our marriage, there were times I was so sure I was right and she was wrong, probably because she was thinking emotionally. But several times, the future proved she was right and I was wrong.

It was natural for us, on the south side of Chicago, to attend Wilson Junior College, which was, I believe, later called Chicago

Teachers College, and then Kennedy King College. It was located at 69th St. and Stewart Avenue. It was virtually free, except for a small fee, perhaps twenty-five dollars, or so. I took general courses at first—social science, English, college algebra, trigonometry, etc. I remember two English teachers there. One of them was quite upset with me when I wrote a paper on whether weightlifting would make you muscle-bound or not. He thought I should have picked a more important subject. But he seemed to like another one I did about my mother's house cleaning. She started slow, but once she got going, like a juggernaut, you couldn't stop her. For the other teacher, I wrote a poem as a report on several English poets. I boldly said in the poem, that Lord Byron "gave himself to the flesh." That was my assessment of him. My teacher did not say anything about it, but I felt that he knew that I was a Christian, and he was not.

After this first year at Wilson, I joined the Army for one year. Upon returning, I decided to take premed courses, as I thought I might become an osteopath or even an M.D. So I took biology, zoology, chemistry, etc. My zoology lab partner happened to be an African American who came to my house a couple of times, as we were studying the parts of a cat's body. My parents had no objections **yet**.

CONTINUING MY EDUCATION

I finished three years at Wilson, which was only supposed to be a two-year school because I was now set to be a missionary, knowing that God could heal. My premed course was discontinued, and I took courses such as literature, writing, and psychology. I had decided the Baptist college in southern Illinois was too liberal. On the other hand, Wheaton College was recommended by my Aunt Matilda, who knew a teacher there. But I wondered if I was ready for a school as conservative as Wheaton. Then, I met a young man from the college, who saw my dilemma and said, "Don't, worry, I had some doubts too, but they put on their pants, one leg at a time, just like we do." (We were both American Baptists.) So I went ahead and applied for summer school, thinking that it might be easier to get in, *but* I was not accepted!

So I went to Champaign-Urbana, the home of the University of Illinois, to see if I could enroll through their fraternity rushing, a procedure by which prospective students visited fraternities to see whether they liked the frats and, vice-versa, whether the frats liked the prospective students. I was not very interested in the fraternities, but at that time, it was very difficult to be enrolled because of so many people trying to get in.

I only remember one of the four frats I "rushed." That was because my cousin, Art Wachholz Jr., had been a member there. Art had been captain of the Morgan Park High School baseball team. He was such an outstanding player that he had a tryout with the Chicago Cubs. *But* that was after he joined the Army and froze his feet in the Battle of the Bulge in WW2, and he was not accepted. And *I wasn't accepted either*, by any of the fraternities.

But while I was preparing to go home, I got a call from my brother, Bill. He was coming down to see if he could get enrolled at the University of Illinois. But the problem was it was so overcrowded, that prospective students could not find housing. And of course, it was no use enrolling, if you didn't have a place to live.

Every place we went was filled up. Finally, we went to the Gym Annex, which they were using for housing because of the overcrowding. But even there, we were told that there were no vacancies. *Then an amazing thing happened!* Although Bill was a veteran Marine and had spent time in China, instead of invading Tokyo, as they were told, he was not known as a smooth persuasive talker, but he replied, "That is too bad! I would have liked to play ball with you guys." (He was speaking of their Intramural Sports program.) The student in charge said, "Just a minute. Let me check."

He came back and said, "There is just one opening." So Bill stayed, and I went home! But don't feel sorry for me! I applied again at Wheaton and was *accepted!* It was all God's work! And Bill was true to his word. The Annex's six-man touch football team won the school Intramural Championship with Bill as receiver and the passer being the two most valuable players!

Meanwhile, I attended the Illinois Institute of Technology for one semester, taking such courses as genetic psychology and economics. I also started another psychology course, but dropped out in the first week. It involved working experiments on mice. I felt like the Lord was saying, "No!" I didn't want to get that involved. Incidentally, the teacher for the genetic psych class was a niece of Sigmund Freud, the inventor and promoter of psychoanalysis. But the class was profitable anyway as we had a text book to follow.

WHEATON

All in all, I enjoyed my two years at Wheaton College very much. It was a stabilizing time in my academic, as well as spiritual, life. It was a conservative Christian school.

Just before beginning there, I had an experience with my cousin, Shirley Wachholz Lombard, Aunt Tillie's daughter (and sister of Art Wachholz, mentioned above). Shirley had a skin disease, which stood in the way of her ambition to be a school teacher. But somehow, she went to a Nazarine Church, where they believed in healing through the Lord Jesus Christ, as the Bible teaches. Praise God! *Her skin was healed*, and she became a school teacher. Later, she went to a Full Gospel Church and received the Baptism of the Holy Spirit, as depicted in the second chapter of the Book of Acts. She told me I needed to be filled with the Spirit of God, and I believed it.

I wondered if I should go ahead and enter Wheaton College after that, for I felt that the Baptism in the Holy Spirit was more important than education. *Yet* I went ahead, and I went seeking for spiritual fulfillment. In addition to daily chapel services with special speakers, as well as Dr. V. Raymond Edman, Wheaton's president, and other leaders, every semester started with a week of special meetings, Starting with A.W. Tozer of Chicago (my cousins used to play with his children in Beverly Hills), also

Harold John Ockenga from Boston's Park Street Church, Richard Seume, and George Sheffer, of Young Life. It seemed to me that these speakers were emphasizing the work and place of the Holy Spirit in our lives, and I was seeking Him with all my heart.

It is so many years ago, as I look back, but it was either Ockenga or Seume, I can't remember which, told the story of a man who had a pet imp of some kind, growing out of his shoulder. He knew it wasn't right or natural, and he should get rid of "him." But he hesitated because the imp was now part of his very body and life. I believe the Lord came to him and presented a way of extinguishing the imp, who pleaded and begged him not to hurt him or take him out of his life. God, on the other hand, told him it was up to him to make the decision. He would not die, but that "thing" that was troubling him would be gone forever, if he just let God deal with it and take it out of his life. Finally, the man made the decision to let God touch the unnatural spot in his body and life and take it away, and when He did, the imp transformed into a beautiful stallion, upon which he could ride away to *victory*! It might sound *sensational* or *corny* to some, but it was not, the way the man of God told it. I don't remember all the details of the story, but it had a profound effect on me. The "imp" represents, of course, the "*flesh*" or some habit or stronghold in our lives, that we hate to let go or give up because it has become part of us. But when we do! There will be a new strength, a new holiness, **victory** in our lives. You could also use this story as an illustration of the consecration needed to receive the Baptism of the Holy Spirit, which I was seeking. I did not realize it then, but it would be more than a decade before that great infilling would be a reality in my life!

When I arrived at Wheaton and went to register, I was in a turmoil. I had gotten interested in philosophy from literature classes but also favored psychology for a major. I walked around the registration area and prayed. Then I noticed that one teacher seemed to be teaching all the psychology courses, so I decided I would rather have more than one teacher for my major classes, so I chose philosophy. I never regretted it. I felt it was a good background for the ministry.

I allowed the various philosophies to try my Christian faith. I said to myself, "Could Immanuel Kant be right? Could Descartes be right? Could Spinoza be right?" By the time I got my degree, I decided, and knew, there was no way to explain the world, with evil and justice manifested, but by the simple explanation of the Bible, particularly the Book of Genesis!

To prove that I was no brilliant student, just a plodder, to get my work done, my grade-point average at Wheaton was listed as only 1.18 and my class rank was 349 out of 379, which means that only 30 of my classmates, out of almost 380, had lower grades than I. So you see, I had nothing to be proud about, yet I was glad to be a graduate of that school!

Before leaving Wheaton, please let me tell you that I believe some of the best things I learned were not from the classrooms but from the library books—for example, *Deeper Experiences of Famous Christians* by James Gilchrist Lawson. The deeper experiences he mentioned were the Baptisms of the Holy Spirit. Although he did not usually explain how they received it, he apparently assumed it, from their lives.

Some of the Christians he mentioned were not so famous, or at least, I didn't know of them. But now I do know them, e.g., Girolama Savonarola, who became one of my heroes. He was a Roman Catholic priest in Italy, who preached against the ruling class of the times, the Medici. He would preach so hard and emotionally that he often had to go to bed for several days to recover. The Hierarchy of the church tried to eliminate him by the method, which we would call today, "kicking him upstairs." That is, they offered him a promotion to the office of cardinal. Savonarola replied, "*The only red hat I desire is the red hat of a martyr!*"

Another hero I read about was John Tauler, the monk who preached to the nuns. But one day, he could not preach but only cried. He was so humiliated that he went to his superior or mentor, who told him, "Tauler, you must die!" He did not mean physical death, but that he must die to self (Gal. 2:20; John 12:24). For many months, Tauler did not preach but sought the Lord for this spiritual death, until he finally came to this place of humility and dependence only upon God. Then, when he again preached to the nuns, it was with great power and anointing.

Later, I found another hero, or rather heroine, the one called Mother Teresa. Some might say that a Roman Catholic should not be my heroine, and it has been said that later in life, she had doubts about her own salvation. My answer to that is that the Roman Church does not seem to uphold the teaching that one can know for sure that he or she is bound for heaven, although the Word of God *does* teach so! (1 John 5:9–13, particularly v. 13, "*These things have I written unto you that believe on the name of the Son of God, that ye may know that ye have eternal life.*" [KJV].) Although that church holds some of the same truths that Evangelical Christians do, there certainly are errors, which we will not discuss in this book. But the Roman church was all that Teresa held as her authority.

I don't think I will ever forget watching a documentary telecast of Teresa and her work in India, shortly before her death. It seemed she could not care less about all the photography and talk about her work. She wanted to minister to "the least of these, my brethren," (Matt. 25:40) to the lowest of the low, to the low-caste people who were dying and had no one to care for them. Her statement tells it all: "I treat every person as if they are Jesus." I would like to quote her poem, "*Anyway,*" here. Some have called it "author unknown." But my information is that it was written or said by Teresa:

> *People are often unreasonable, illogical, and*
> *self-centered. Forgive them, anyway.*
> *If you are kind, people may accuse you of*
> *selfish, ulterior motives. Be kind, anyway.*
> *If you are successful, you will win some false friends*
> *and some true enemies. Be successful, anyway.*
> *If you are honest and frank, people may cheat*
> *you. Be honest and frank, anyway.*
> *If you find serenity and happiness, they*
> *may be jealous. Be happy, anyway.*

*What you do today, people will often forget
tomorrow. Do good, anyway.
Give the world the best you have, and it may never be
enough. Give the world the best you've got, anyway.
You see, in the final analysis, it is between you and
God, it was never between you and them, anyway.*

Another of my Heroes of the Faith was Sadhu Sundar Singh, brought up to be an Indian Holy Man by his mother, but when she died, his world collapsed. A Christian tried to give him a Bible, but he would have none of it. So he began fasting to "find God" but was despondent when there was no spiritual manifestation. Finally, he decided he would throw himself on the railroad tracks and commit suicide, if he did not find God in one more day. And suddenly Jesus appeared to him (as He is appearing to many Muslims today in dreams).

His ministry began now as a *Christian* Holy Man. He became so popular that he made trips to England and America, telling Westerners that their materialism was thwarting their spiritual lives. By this time, Sundar was a bearded man. And the story was told about him, in visiting a home in America, a child came to the door. Upon seeing Sundar, he ran back to his parents, crying that "Jesus is at the door!"

Returning to India, he began making trips to Tibet to bring the Gospel there. It was dangerous, mountainous terrain. After his last trip, he was never heard from again, but his bloody trail was found in the mountains of Tibet, hence he is known as the Disciple of the Bleeding Feet.

All these heroes I found in the library at Wheaton, except Mother Teresa. And there were others, such as John Huss and Martin Luther. But I have had to add another Roman Catholic, in late years, Immaculée Ilibagiza (*Left to Tell, Discovering God Amidst the Rwandan Holocaust*, Immaculée Ilibagiza with Steve Erwin, Hay House. Inc., 2006).

A college student, she could not go home for Christmas because of the Hutu tribe killing of the Tutsis, but she was hidden by a Protestant Hutu Pastor in a small bathroom for three months with five other females. All she could do was pray, perhaps to the Virgin Mary but also to Jesus! At one point, she said, "I heard myself speaking in an exotic language." She lost forty pounds during the ordeal and weighed only sixty-five pounds when released (Ilibagiza, p. 107). She also stated that she prayed fifteen to twenty hours a day and was born again in the bathroom. Later, she immigrated to the United States, married, had two children, and worked for the United Nations in New York (Ibid, p. 134).

Other schools I attended were Loyola University, Chicago State University, and Governor State University—in all of which I took education classes, as I spent a few years teaching in Chicago public schools and a Christian school (where I met my wife-to-be).

But before I even met her, probably the most important part of my education as a minister, took place. People often joke about and call a theological seminary a "cemetery," but I am most thankful for my three years at Northern Baptist, under godly teachers, as well as my quarter at Fuller, in Pasadena, California, 1954–1959, in all.

NORTHERN BAPTIST THEOLOGICAL SEMINARY

At Northern, I took yearlong Bible courses, covering the Old and New Testaments; Greek courses covering the whole New Testament; plus elective courses in Romans, Jeremiah, Psalms, and Luke; Pauline, Petrine, and Johanine Theology; Christian Education; Church History; Baptist Church History; Baptist Missions; Doctrines of Creation; Revelation; and Redemption; Evangelism; Bible, Personal, and Parish; Church Music, Homiletics (Preaching) Expository; from Bible Characters; Sermon Preparation; and Delivery.

In the middle of my second year at Northern, I left school and drove to California, still seeking for the Baptism of the Holy Spirit. While there, I enrolled in Fuller Seminary in Pasadena, which I enjoyed, taking courses in both homiletics and speech, plus a noteworthy class in systematic theology, on epistemology (How we know things spiritually) taught by Edward J. Carnell, president of the school (also a Wheaton grad). He taught that there are only two equal ways to please God—by doing His will or by being spontaneously sorry for *not* doing it, i.e., repenting, which he called the boon of the Reformation.

However, after just one quarter at Fuller, I was called to return to Chicago to help take care of my father who suffered a stroke. But later, I returned to Northern and finished the course for the required Bachelor of Divinity degree.

CHAPTER 6

SECULAR AND CHRISTIAN WORK

Secular work—by *secular*, I mean it was working for paychecks, not for churches or Christian organizations.

FULL-TIME WORK

In my twenties, I got a job at Kroger's Bakery on the south side of Chicago. (The building was later transformed into Simeon High School, which produced some excellent athletic teams.) We stacked the bread and trays from an assembly line and had to work very fast. An African American man, a little older than I, showed me just how to do it.

Eventually, I invited him to a Pentecostal Church, where my cousin, Shirley, was preaching. I wondered why he didn't show up. He said he went there but was afraid to go in. That is both *good* and *bad*. It was bad that he did not go in. Some storefront churches, at least, in those days, used to broadcast their services to the street. He probably heard the music and shouting. Something was going on! It was not just a quiet church, like he may have been used to. People are afraid of the supernatural!

I remember, a little later, when I went to the Mason Temple (named after the founder of the Church of God in Christ), I saw a young man suddenly rise in the Spirit, at least a foot or two off the floor from a sitting position. You can become afraid of God or investigate and see what it is all about. I was investigating in those days. God works in the lives of His people. Even in the Old Testament, we see God working in the lives of the prophets!

I also got a job at the old main post office in downtown Chicago. (I had previously worked, delivering mail on foot at Christmastime in my late teens.)

It seems that everywhere I worked, I befriended African Americans, also a young Hispanic man, in this case. And then a Caucasian man, who turned out to be a homosexual. He also came to one or two of our church services, later when I was pastor of a Baptist church in Chicago. He was a Roman Catholic and made it a point to let me know that he prayed to Mary. Finally, I saw his situation, which I believe is like most homosexuals—his father seemed to be a stern man that was either absent or he could not be pleased by his son. So the son clung to his mother and sister and sought to be like them.

HOMOSEXUALITY

I have come across several "gays" in my life, most of them in California, for some reason. I never had anything against them, except that I knew their lifestyle was not pleasing to God. (See Lev. 18:22, Gen. 19:4–28.) There was the guy who kept staring at me, day after day, in the shower room of the gym we attended. I assumed, it was because he was "gay." Then there was the Central American who kissed me under the influence of alcohol, crying that there was no hope for him. (Of course, I tried to tell him otherwise.)

Another, rather strong appearing young man, wanted to give me a back massage. Then he pulled down the shade in my room. I discerned he had something other in mind than a back massage, so I told him to leave. And he did. It did not seem to be the time to preach to him.

Another one came into the YMCA, where I was staying. Somehow the subject of the "gay" lifestyle came up, so I read to him from Romans 1:24–27. God seemed to touch his heart. He said I was going to be his first victim, but now, God had stopped him. He said he had to leave then. But when I tried to find him later, I was told he had checked out, although he had just come into the hotel. I had wanted to help him a little more from the Word of God, but trust he was already on his way of coming to our Savior.

I had two "bosses" whom I was told were "gay." One was a supervisor in the employment service; the other was a school principal. Of course, I never said a word to them, but respected them, and tried to be obedient to whatever they told me to do. In summary, we Christians love everyone but do not condone wrong and immoral lifestyles.

Almighty God, our Father and Creator, established the first institution for mankind—*marriage and the family*—in such a beautiful and loving plan. He made a helper for Adam—Eve, taken from Adam's own body in the world's first surgery, by God. Adam said, "*This is now bone of my bone, and flesh of my flesh…therefore a man shall leave his father and mother and be joined to his wife, and they shall become one flesh*" (Gen. 2:20–24). It is an abomination and irreverence to God to say we now have an alternative lifestyle, just as good as God's Plan, and it is politically incorrect and intolerant, if you do not accept man's way, instead of God's way!

WHAT TO DO IF YOUR BOSS OR FELLOW WORKERS SHOW THEY DON'T LIKE YOU

I always tried my best to be a good employee and paid no attention to the thought I was being treated unjustly by my bosses or fellow employees. I tried all the harder to be a good employee. When I worked for the state of Illinois Employment Security, just after the Unemployment Compensation Department merged with Job Service, some of we JS people, through the union, were given jobs as adjudicators (small-time judges who decided whether applicants for unemployment compensation would receive benefits or not). The atmosphere of the office was like *ice*, as the unemployment people were mad because we had taken some of their jobs.

But I just tried my best to please the management bosses, who were unemployment people, by staying overtime, coming in on holidays to keep my caseload down. I made friends of these bosses, by treating them with respect and obedience. I got along fine, and they seemed to love me for it. For they saw I wasn't afraid to work. (I got paid for it!) I worked over twenty-one years for the State of Illinois Employment Security and don't know what I and my family would do without the pension I receive, as well as Social Security. *I thank God for it!*

In California, I worked on an assembly line, putting mixed fruit in cans. I met some interesting people there, including an ex-drug addict, who compared the addiction to a religion.

California gave their workers good benefits, so they only worked about six months in the summer season and collected unemployment compensation the rest of the year. I heard Ronald Reagan speak, in person, while there. I think he was campaigning for senator Barry Goldwater for the 1960 election. Little did I or anyone know he would later become governor of California and even president of our country!

There was a great demand for teachers in the 1960s, so I began teaching under a provisional certificate with the Chicago Board of Education (later to be called the Chicago Public Schools). I worked in several schools, and then took a sixth-grade class, after Bettye and I were married, near the "projects," the tall apartment buildings on the near south side—Williams School. It was very difficult. The desks were not stationary. At the end of the day, many of the books would be on the floor. Sometimes, the students would put tacks on my seat, when I wasn't looking. They even threw things at me. I was determined to work with the black students, but was not very successful.

I tried to get one boy to sit down by putting my hand on his shoulder. *"Don't touch me!"* he shouted. He must have gone home at lunchtime and told his uncle he was being mistreated. Luckily, or perhaps, providentially, the master teacher intercepted him before he could get to me because he was angry and ready to fight me until he was told that his nephew refused to sit in his seat.

At the end of that semester, I had a chance to aid another teacher in TESLing (teaching English as a second language to Hispanic students). It was all arranged, but then, I changed my mind. The TESLing position would have been much easier, but somehow, I felt I should continue with my black students. Was it a mistake?

Possibly, because after one more semester, I was ready to take a position with Job Service for much less money, which was a hardship for beginning a family. But as already mentioned, I stayed with the state of Illinois for over twenty-one years. I pastored several churches while working for the state. It was not easy but was necessary for support of our family, as well as my personal spiritual development.

It was important for me to help people with my work. And I realized it was very important to help people find jobs or to get training so they could work.

FULL-TIME TELEMARKETING

When we moved to Dallas, Texas (by prophecy, to be explained later), I did full-time telemarketing for various companies, including an airline and later business services for CEOs. It was difficult at times because I got a case of bronchitis in some unusual icy weather. But I kept on working. *I thank the Lord for that.*

PART-TIME WORK SELLING ENCYCLOPEDIAS

I sold both *World Books* and *Encyclopedia Britannica* (not at the same time). *World Books* were easier to sell as they cost less and were adequate for most people. I sold just enough of them to get a free set of *Childcraft* (for children) and later a set of *World Books* free. I became famous to our family by answering their questions, saying, "Look it up in your *Childcraft*" and later, "Look it up in the *World Book*." They thought I said this because I didn't know the answer to their questions, but that was not necessarily so. I wanted them to get in the habit of finding the answers for themselves. Of course, today, our grandchildren do not need encyclopedias, when they have the World Wide Web on their computers or smart phones.

I must mention my boss in selling the *Britannica*. He was an African American man who insisted we get dressed up and put on shoes in the a.m., even if we only call prospects on the phone, so we won't get and feel too comfortable.

He was all business, but don't you dare bother him on Sundays, at least in the fall. He was a Green Bay Packer fan, watching the games on TV with his whole family. And he almost idolized Curly Lambeau, the Packers' coach.

TELEMARKETING

I worked for Mastercraft, selling siding and other home improvements. We did not actually make sales on the phone but sought to make appointments for our salesmen with the homeowners. I only had one appointment resulting in a sale, but that was a whole home siding, costing about $1,000. I got a $100 bonus—otherwise, I was still paid by the hours I worked.

I would work from 5 to 9 p.m. I was a "brown bagger." Most of the time, I worked bringing peanut butter or cold meat sandwiches and an apple, or perhaps a few cookies, with me. Because

I worked at night, I brought two lunches to work. Although busy, I was happy, feeling I was helping my family with the extra money.

Later, I worked for Sears and several other telemarketing companies, including soliciting funds for police organizations.

In the early part of our marriage, Saturdays found me working as an oculist for Marshall Fields, straightening glasses that did not fit, as a service to customers. I would put the glasses in hot sand to soften them up before attempting to bend the stems back to their original shape. We lived in the high-rise at 20th and Michigan at the time, and I would walk to work, about twenty blocks, as there was no place to park downtown. I also took measurements of the customers' faces in ordering glasses for them.

MINISTERIAL WORK

Pastoring churches, working as an evangelist, hospital and nursing home work, Youth for Christ [Club and Rally Director] and other witnessing.

Pastorates—The first one was in the rural area near Guthrie, Oklahoma, the Abell Community Church. I had been in Oklahoma before, at Fort Sill (while in military service), in the southern part, near Lawton. Guthrie was a few miles south of Oklahoma City. I was sent there through Wheaton College. It was farm country, and I lived on the farm of Donald Coffin and his wife. Donald was a college grad who raised hogs and other animals.

The church had been established by the American Sunday School Union, whose leader was not able to hold services every Sunday, hence, a full-time pastor was needed. I was thankful for the opportunity, as the only preaching I had done was in missions and some street preaching.

I had some chores assigned to me, a city boy, on a farm for the first time. I first tried to milk "Daisy" but was not too successful. So I was given another job, feeding the sows.

They were the mother hogs, which probably averaged at least four hundred pounds each! My duty was to pour cereal grain from a bucket into their troughs. But the catch was doing it before they bit my knees! They didn't mean me any harm, but they were so hungry that my knees were in danger! I say knees because I wore knee-length rubber boots to protect my legs. The solution was that I tried to feed them at a slightly different time, every day. Otherwise, I would have a mob of hungry sows ganging up on me every day, and I'd never get to the feeding troughs!

One more terrible problem must be mentioned. I was given a small, one-room wooden house in which to live. The problem was that a skunk, somehow, got into the wall of the place and was living there. The stench was bad!

I don't remember who it was, but they got someone with a shotgun, who shot and killed the villain skunk! Only, now I had another problem. The stink was so bad that I had to move out for a few days! I don't remember where I went, but finally, I moved back in. Such were the challenges of a city boy in the country!

Yet another problem was harvest time. The dedicated Christians would take Sundays off, from their work with the big machines. Others would not. They would work on Sundays and not come to church.

We had a vacation Bible school. Several accepted Christ as their Savior. We baptized them in a lake. One sainted old lady with a Presbyterian background said, "Dick [they called me by my first name] will baptize you anyway you want," i.e., by immersion or sprinkling. But with my Baptist background, I disagreed with her, saying, "No, I can't do that." To me, baptism meant "immersion." That was the only way that the beautiful symbolism of Christ, dying for our sins and then being resurrected, *and* our dying to our old life of sin, and rising out of the water to a *new* life in Christ, could be portrayed.

I also preached a one-week revival at a neighboring country church. Several teenage girls were giggling and talking during one service, but when the invitation was given, they came forward to accept Our Lord Jesus Christ as Savior.

While at Abell, I also had the opportunity to have a radio program. Sometimes, we had children or others singing, but I always got the chance to preach. And some of the people of the area got to know me.

All in all, I enjoyed this, my first pastorate, learning to preach by experience. Some of the men of the church smoked tobacco. I don't remember that I preached against it, but I did let them know that I didn't approve. I was somewhat of a legalist in that respect and didn't know how to handle it. I met with the elders of the church and told them I felt I should leave the church. They reluctantly agreed. I had been there since November, 1959. It was now 1960 or 1961.

YOUTH FOR CHRIST

Sometime in the 1950s, I started attending YFC rallies on Saturday nights. I didn't drive until I was thirty years old, when my father gave me his old '59 Chevy Impala. So I would take the "L" or buses downtown to Orchestra Hall, where the rallies were held.

As I said, I lacked assurance of salvation in those days. I remember very well, one night after the rally, I was approached by a young man, maybe in his thirties, wearing a white clergy collar. I assumed he was a Lutheran minister. He asked me if I was saved. I answered, "I don't know. I think I am."

He replied, "It's not a guessing game" and walked away, disgusted.

YFC was started by Torey Johnson. At least, he was the first president. In those days, I would say most people came to Christ through Sunday schools, Evangelist Billy Graham Crusades, or Youth for Christ. Billy Graham. By the way, was YFC's first full-time employee.

Gene Mcgee, a southerner from Georgia, took over Chicagoland YFC about that time. He was a veteran who had worked with servicemen, giving them Bible-based lessons by correspondence to get them grounded in the Lord. This I found out when I volunteered to help him and worked as a file clerk.

In 1957, I went to the Youth for Christ Leadership School in Kansas City, under Al Metsker, who was the rally director there. On the last day, the morning prayer meeting lasted until afternoon. The Spirit of God was speaking to hearts, and the students were confessing their sins. But strangely, God seemed to be telling me that YFC was not for me, although at that time I learned a lot and was very interested in the work!

As I write now, sixty years later, I can't remember the details and time frame, but when I was in California, I talked with the director of Los Angeles YFC, Jim McKeown. He was going to hire me as a club director and get me a car. I was to meet with him after a rally in Long Beach. But the rally lasted so long, I was afraid I would not be able to get the last bus back to La Puente, where I was staying. I never went back, concluding that if it was God's will, it would have worked out.

But four years later, I attended another YFC leadership school at Green Lake, Wisconsin, under Carl (Kelly) Bihl, our music director, as well as teacher. This time I was appointed as director of YFC at Dodge City, Kansas.

My office was on Wyatt Earp Blvd., in the office of a young Christian attorney, Don Schultz, who was very good to me. My job was to obtain speakers, special music, and plan and conduct the weekly Saturday night rally. I also sent out letters and visited people, attempting to raise funds for the work.

While there, I was told about a tough kid, of whom, even the police were afraid. He was said to have hit one of the policemen in the jaw and knocked him out. From what I heard, I was afraid to "tackle" this guy, but knew I must. He lived with his grandfather. I fearfully went to his house but finally met him, and I believe, I won his respect. He told me some of the wild, sinful things, he and others used to do. I tried to give him some good advice. I had a barbell and used to lift weights with him and another young fellow. I can't say I led him to the Lord, but I tried.

I went to a Salvation Army Church one Sunday night, where a homeless young teenage boy came to the altar. Since he had nowhere to go, I took him into my basement apartment. Later, I took him with me to a camp near Colorado Springs, for "juvenile delinquents," as they called them, in those days.

They had a wrestling mat there, and having been on the wrestling team in high school, I wrestled with a couple of the boys, taking it easy with them because they knew little about wrestling. But when my boy had his turn with me, he seemed to be determined that he could beat me, little as he was. I had to wrestle him hard and pin him!

I got him a job, but, unfortunately, day after day, he refused to go to work. I couldn't watch him all day, not knowing what he was going to do. I finally had to call a relative to come and get him. Again, I tried to help, but apparently failed.

I told the area director, who had hired me, that I felt like I was in the wrong place. Somehow, I thought he was going to encourage me to keep on. He did not. He already had someone to take my place. You can see I was unstable in those days! But better days were yet to come!

BETHANY BAPTIST CHURCH

Again, I was assigned to a church through Wheaton College's placement service. (Thank God for Wheaton!) And now I was only a few miles from my home on the south side of Chicago. The church was a large old church, which needed and got a "face lifting" while I was there. (We had the outside bricks sandblasted, so they looked like new.) It was at 35th St. and Hoyne Avenue, an old German, Irish, maybe some Polish, neighborhood. There were some Hispanics around 35th St. Today it is probably almost totally Hispanic.

I was there only about one year. It was a Conservative Baptist Church. The Conservative Baptist movement caused a split in American Baptist churches, starting some twenty years before. I agreed with them wholeheartedly, as far as biblical doctrine goes, but I was still seeking and believing in the Baptism of the Holy Spirit, which will be taken up more thoroughly in the next chapter. But thank God, I did receive the great infilling, while pastoring at Bethany.

I believe my preaching had an impact on the young people of the church. I started a Boys Club on a weekday evening and had some big crowds. Unfortunately, some of the boys were literally "from the other side of the tracks."

A young Jewish Christian man donated a wrestling mat for the club. However, unbeknownst to me, someone spray-painted graffiti on the basement walls, where our club took place. My board of deacons insisted we could not have a club, which caused that kind of trouble. I had to agree with them, reluctantly. But we probably had more teenage boys attending the club, than members attending church, so I hated to see them told they could no longer come to the club and have a chance to know the Savior!

I continued visitation on the other side of the tracks, across Damen Avenue. I befriended an Italian American family, including their son, about sixteen years old.

One Sunday, the mother, dressed to the hilt, walked into the church. It may have been her first time in a church! Later, one of the deaconesses said she saw the boy with a cigarette in his mouth. But she was wrong! It was only a pencil in his mouth.

Everyone remembers where they were when President Kennedy was killed. I was out doing visitation, counseling a man who was trying to kick the tobacco habit. Then I talked to his wife and realized my counseling was inadequate because I was a single man and knew nothing, by experience, about marriage.

Two other events happened while at Bethany. I had an ordination council meeting. I had just graduated from Northern Baptist Seminary, so I felt I was ready, but was afraid they would question me about the Baptism of the Holy Spirit, which I believed in, but had not yet experienced.

They asked me questions, like "What is the definition of a pastor?" "How many books do you have in your library?" I answered, "It is right there," And I pointed to my office, saying, "You can see for yourselves." No one took me up on it.

Then they took a vote and told me I did not make it. My reaction? I said to myself, *I am no longer a Baptist*. Then the area Baptist superintendent said that I should study and outline every chapter in the New Testament. I started to do as he advised. But never finished. Remember, I had just been graduated from the Baptist Seminary. The courses I took there, covering the whole Bible, were listed in an earlier chapter. (I think the reason they did not OK me was that they were so extremely conservative, that even Billy Graham, for instance, was too liberal for them.)

The other "event" I mentioned was that when I finally told my board of deacons (led by one young man, just back from the war in Vietnam) I had received the Baptism of the Spirit, they demanded that I resign because I had left Baptist doctrine and practice. I did resign but insisted that I did *not* depart from Baptist doctrine because *Baptist doctrine* is the New Testament, and I surely did not depart from the NT because the Baptism of the Holy Spirit is plainly put forth, particularly, in the book of Acts. They did not like my saying so, at all.

I was told they had arranged for a debate between me and a teacher from Moody Bible Institute, about the Baptism of the Holy Spirit. But in the end, the teacher changed his mind and withdrew his acceptance.

GOSPEL FELLOWSHIP TABERNACLE

After Bettye and I were married, we both had "papers" as evangelists or ministers of the United Pentecostal Council of the Assemblies of God, with headquarters near Boston, Massachusetts. This was a black denomination of Pentecostal churches, formed out of the Assemblies of God, a largely white group of churches, because it was felt that the white group was prejudiced and discriminated against their black brothers. I don't know the details of the movement. But it included churches in several parts of the country, particularly in the east, and also in the West Indies area.

Under the guidance of Elder Hall, of the "Council," we were given the opportunity of using the basement of an apartment building to begin a church. There had been a church there before, under Pastor Fitz Barclay, who was now our pastor at the Progressive Beulah Pentecostal Church, at 87th and Throop. We had left the church, under which we had met and married, Evangelical Christian Church, and school, because we had charges against the pastor.

We did a lot of work together, Bettye and I, scrubbing and painting the walls and floors before beginning the church. It was a time of bonding, as we worked together, for the glory of God. The colors we used were white, blue, and green. Each of the colors meant something—white for holiness, blue for heaven (the spiritual color), and green for growth in our Christian lives.

We invited the people we knew and soon had a congregation, not a lot, but some. Eventually, we had Sunday school classes for the children. We canvassed the neighborhood. But I don't remember anyone coming, as a result. A little earlier, Bettye and I went on a campaign to witness to as many people as we could, hopefully to win forty people to the Lord. We went to the beaches at the Lakefront, in our neighborhood, wherever we could. God did bless to bring forty to the Lord, but we had no church, in which to invite them, and it was difficult to follow up on them. That is when we decided to start a church.

On Sundays, we would go to church, I would preach, and we would come home, tired, and would go to bed and read the Sunday paper. I remember it as a happy time.

But as stated in the title of this memoir, I must also make my confessions. The time came, I think after a year or two as pastor, I felt the Lord was leading me to resign from the church. The reason was that according to such Scripture passages as 1 Timothy 3:4, 5 and Titus 1:6, I did not always have my house and my children under control, which is required for a pastor.

I did not really consider our children as boisterous, but some in the congregation accused them of disturbing our worship. It was a humbling thing for me to do, but I felt, before God, that I really did not show the character of a pastor. In fact, after much prayer, I came to the place where I believed that my main calling was not that of a pastor, but of an evangelist.

Therefore, I made my resignation and appointed a young man, Louis Isaac, to take my place as pastor. He was faithful and, I believe, did well as pastor. He married Sharon Hicks, a young lady, who had led the choir in our "Mother Church," Progressive Beulah. They had several children, and Sharon made them into a musical group that served at many churches.

However, after I resigned, a young lady, the wife of an evangelist in our church, came to our door and told me that "the captain must not give up the ship" (i.e., the church). She was very sincere, and I took her words to heart. But I had prayed a long time before making my decision, and I stayed with it.

Before leaving the Gospel Fellowship Tabernacle, I should say it was an ordeal for Bettye, as well as me. Her call to preach had come to a "head" in the difficult birth of our son, David, our second child. He suffered a broken collar bone in the birth. But more than that, the church in which she grew up did not acknowledge women preachers. Bettye tells in her own book *Through Much Tribulation We Shall Overcome*, how a friend told her, after David's birth, that she was called to preach (p. 117) and our own pastor had just told her that she was "sitting down" on her calling.

She never told me at that time, but Bettye was fasting three days a week because it was so hard for her to "be a pastor's wife." She came to the church every Wednesday morning to pray with whoever would come. But some of the people wanted her to take them here, there, or everywhere, and she would do it without telling them she was fasting. So it was difficult for her. Yes, she was called to preach, *but a Pastor's wife*? She could not handle it. Years later, she felt it was *not* God's will for her to fast so much. It was *religion*, which no doubt weakened her already frail body.

RICHARD WESLEY LYTHBERG

PARK FOREST FULL GOSPEL CHURCH

Looking back, it is hard for me to reconcile the "pioneering" of yet another church after leaving the last one because I was an evangelist rather than a pastor. But this was all we knew, going out and evangelizing door-to-door, or anywhere. But then, we had to have somewhere to follow up with any new converts.

So Bettye gave me one year to go out canvassing the neighborhood, seeking to win souls, on Saturdays, my day off. But I didn't go every Saturday; sometimes there was yardwork or basement work. By that time, we had bought a house in Roseland, on the corner of 120th Street, paying only $20,000. (But at that time, it was not a small amount.)

We moved in, in the winter, thinking it was a mixed neighborhood. In the spring, when everyone came out of their houses, we found it was a black neighborhood. Of course, it made no difference to us, except that we thought that a mixed neighborhood would be best for our kids.

One day, a young guy, maybe a teenager, came at me, as I was crossing the street, saying, "What have you got?" with one hand out to take my money, if I had any, and his other hand in his pocket, bulging out, like he had a gun. I was scared to death. But I yelled, "I haven't got anything!" and started running as fast as I could. As I looked back, I saw him make a throwing motion, like he was throwing a knife, but he didn't throw anything.

If he had a gun, he could have shot me! Thank God! This was one of many times the Lord protected me! I thought he lived across the street, but I never saw him again. But I was so scared, I ran about two blocks before circling back to our house.

Later, we moved to University Park, which was first called Park Forest South. So I went back to Park Forest and rented a schoolroom for Sunday morning services. This time, we did have more of a mixed congregation.

We had a white lady in the congregation who worked for the post office, delivering mail. She asked prayer for her husband, who played a bass guitar at night clubs on Saturday nights, and therefore, never came to church.

However, one Easter (Resurrection Day) service, he came, just as the service was ending. Somehow, I did not feel led to pressure him at that time, for a commitment to Christ, as he apparently had been up all night and was just coming from the night club. But I did go to see him at his house, a day or two later, and led him to the Lord. He was truly saved and followed the Lord, from then on! He once told me, *"I will be eternally grateful to you, for leading me to the Lord."* Praise God! That makes it all worthwhile!

PART TIME CHRISTIAN SERVICE

Some of the happiest times of my life were in my twenties and thirties, going to the "Skid Row Missions," like the Pacific Garden Mission, the Christian Industrial League Mission, and the West Side Rescue Mission, first with Beverly Emmanuel Baptist Church, and then with the Stone Church (Assemblies of God).

After my first two attempts at preaching, at Foster Park Baptist, where I grew up, I started preaching in missions and in street meetings at 63rd and Halsted streets, a well-known shopping center at that time. One of the leaders of the street meetings was Bro. Galloway, who worked for the post office. He was the only one in the church, who, at times, would come out with a big "Amen!" during church services. I liked it!

Let me say, right here, that when I worked for the WIN (work incentive program), trying to prepare people on public aid, for jobs, through training and other means, one of my clients told me about Bob Weeden, who had been in all kinds of crime but had gotten saved when an old lady neighbor persisted in inviting him to church. He finally gave in, went to church and *got saved!* He then went to the police and surrendered and was put in the county jail in Chicago, where he started telling the other prisoners about Jesus. They said, "You can't do that here!" So they sent him to the prison at Joliet. He did the same there, and they sent him to

Menard Prison in Southern Illinois. But he wouldn't stop witnessing! You see, just like the apostle Paul, once he was saved, he was all out for God!

Finally, they saw that his witnessing was doing some good! Prisoners were getting saved! And they weren't giving the guards any more trouble. The prison officials said, "*Mr. Weeden*, we will give you a room, where you can teach the other prisoners!" Praise God! (You see, if we will *keep on,* and will not be discouraged, *God will bless us and open a way for us!*)

Weeden finally applied for a hearing, and the God he now trusted in did a miracle! They could not find any records of the many crimes he committed—counterfeiting, burglaries, hit man, etc. So they had to let him go! After that, he preached at our church twice. He would talk very fast, telling about all his crimes. Why? You might ask. Because he was so glad to be forgiven, and on God's side! He wanted to tell everybody about it!

We held a street meeting at 63rd and Halsted and invited him to come and preach. Which he did, and he told me he recognized *some* of the houses he used to burglarize in that area! Later, he started a street mission, where he took addicts, ex-criminals, etc., in to rehabilitate them and teach them the Word, and then some were sent to farms for further rehab!

One thing I remembered about the Skid Row work was in coming home from the Pacific Garden Mission, on State Street downtown. I was in a car driven by Dan Gallacher, and I made a remark about him being Irish, which I surely thought was true, from his name. He let me know, right away, in no uncertain terms, that he was *not Irish, but Scotch*, and if I mentioned such a thing as that again, I would have to get out of the car and walk!

Later, Dan became president of the mission, succeeding Harry Saulnier, the longtime president. The mission became famous, I believe, through Billy Sunday, formerly, a great Major League ball player, who was saved there and became a great evangelist, plus their weekly radio broadcasts of *Unshackled*, dramatized stories of men who were down and out, addicted to liquor, drugs, etc., finally becoming *unshackled*, delivered and set free from the power of alcohol or whatever was holding them in bondage.

If you are not familiar with how the rescue missions worked, the men, who were reduced to poverty and homelessness by the liquor habit, would come in for a meal, but first would have to listen to a message, designed to lead them to Christ, and set them free from the bondage of sin. And of course, thank God, some would respond to the altar call! After that, some would be taken in and be given a bed for the night. If serious, some would stay weeks or months in Bible teaching classes, to get them grounded in the Word, so they could stand "against the wiles of the Devil" (Eph. 6:11).

Another mission, which operated similarly, was the Christian Industrial League Mission. I believe that is where I had a real *victory* one day. One of my problems in those days were "colds" and sore throats, making it difficult for me to preach, as I was beginning to do. This time, I was much in prayer, fearing I would not be able to preach, due to a cold. But praise God! When I got up to preach, I was enabled to do so, for the first time, under those circumstances!

And when I gave the "invitation," about a dozen men responded, came forward for prayer, and I felt that they were really saved!

Later, I was asked to become a counselor at that mission, which I did, coming once a week, trying to help the men discover just what caused them to drink and encouraging them in their Christian life.

One night, in one of the missions, there was a Negro man sitting with a white woman. Afterward, one of the women, working with the mission, made a remark about how terrible that was. Being yet a young man, I didn't say anything. But I did not see anything wrong with it, as if they were committing fornication or something. I thought the lady who made the statement was a Southerner, as she said, "God has set the bounds," apparently referring to Acts 17:26—"Hath made of one blood all nations of men for to dwell on all the face of the earth, and hath determined the times before appointed, and the bounds of their habitation."

This Scripture does not prove that God approves of segregation, as this lady was probably trying to say. If she meant that "God had determined the bounds of their habitation" meant that Negroes should stay in Africa, then *why did the white race bring them here to America*, away from their place in Africa? (We will speak more on this topic in a later chapter.)

CHRISTIAN AND MISSIONARY ALLIANCE CHURCH AND THE OPEN- AIR CAMPAIGNERS

About this time, I became very interested in the Christian and Missionary Alliance Church, pastored by Dr. A. W. Tozer. I liked the church so much that I wanted to join it. But I was told that I would have to talk to the pastor first. The problem was that he was always in prayer. When I called for an appointment, I was told we could meet at the church, just before the midweek prayer meeting, but he did not show up! So I finally dismissed the idea.

One thing I liked about the church was the Open-Air Campaigners, under Earl Anthony, who came from the United Kingdom. I enjoyed the companionship of the young men who worked with this witnessing endeavor because they were "sold out" to the Lord. Lou Finney seemed to be their leader. Another name I remember was Ray Marshall.

We would go downtown or other places, in the summer, and would hold a service for the men who were eating their lunches outdoors. I think Bro. Anthony did the preaching, but others would give their testimonies.

OTHER PERSONAL WORK

Soon after conversion, I began witnessing to my new faith as best I could. Somehow, I became acquainted with the "Herald of His Coming," a holiness paper which dealt with healing and fasting, but did not seem to be Pentecostal, as far as advocating "speaking with tongues." A couple of the laymen of the Beverly Emmanuel Baptist Church, where I was then a member, were strong for the periodical. Maybe they sent it to me.

I don't remember ringing any doorbells, but after sending for a supply of the papers, I would leave them on the doorknobs in my neighborhood. That was the first time I did anything like that. I must have been in my late teens or early twenties.

I heard a lot of messages about witnessing for Christ and winning souls—in Youth for Christ, WMBI (Moody Bible Institute radio), First Baptist Church of Hammond (Indiana) under Pastor Jack Hyles, and other Baptist churches, so I began doing that, the best way I could. When I traveled by bus, I would ask the person sitting next to me if I could show them a Bible verse or read it to them. John 5:24 was a favorite verse: "*Verily, verily, I say unto you, he who hears my word and believes on him Who sent Me, has everlasting life, and shall not come into condemnation; but is passed from death unto life*" (KJV). I tried to show them that eternal life begins right here and now, if they believe that God sent Jesus to be our Savior (through the blood sacrifice on the cross). I don't remember anyone being saved that way, but most people listened.

I also talked to people on the elevated trains, going to work. They would be so crowded that I and other people had to stand, and I prayed with young men for salvation. And some gave me their addresses for follow up. In later years, at bus stations, sometimes, I would speak loudly, a brief testimony or salvation message and invitation. There was also the *Wordless Book*, mentioned earlier, as a means of leading children to the Lord and salvation.

One of the most important things I did was at Victory Center at 108 N Dearborn, in the "Loop" (downtown Chicago). Several Christian organizations were in the same building, including the Christian Businessmen's Committee (who were very strong on witnessing and soul-winning), the Servicemen's Center, Youth for Christ, and others. The Servicemen's Center catered to sailors from the Great Lakes Naval Station, as well as Army men from

Fort Sheridan. There were two well-experienced ministers there, who knew how to win men to Christ. It was in the days just after the Second World War. I went there on Saturdays at first. Their method was to play checkers or ping-pong with the men and, then afterward, ask them if anyone had ever explained God's plan of salvation to them. Almost without exception, they would reply, "No." So we would show them the Scriptures involved and then lead them in prayer for salvation.

I called it *beginner's luck*, as I tried to do exactly what the experienced men told me to do, and each one had a slightly different plan of salvation. And for seven weeks, I believe it was about five or more men would pray for salvation every week, without any of them rejecting the invitation. Sometimes, I could see their faces change as they prayed. They were in the presence of God, and no longer in my presence! Then, for some reason, I changed my day from Saturday to Sunday, and the spell was broken. I averaged leading only about one man to the Lord each Sunday!

Later, when I was active as an evangelist with the Assemblies of God, I labored to teach churches how to win souls. The plan was, after teaching them for at least one week, they were to go out in their neighborhoods, under their pastor and myself, to witness, and hopefully win souls. But it seemed that the pastors changed their minds and said they were not ready, although we had practiced and should have been ready and prayed up to begin this important work of witnessing and winning souls!

This was very discouraging to me. "*For the Son of man is come to seek and to save that which was lost*" (Luke 19:10, KJV). "*He that winneth souls is wise*" (Prov. 11:30, KJV).

For about the last three years, I have been going door-to-door, starting with my next-door neighbors, trying to bring them to Christ, where ever I lived. The Lord directed me to make a short, half-page tract of my own, making it personal. The method the Lord gave me was to say, "I'm out meeting my neighbors, asking everybody one question—'What do you think is the most important thing in life?'"

Most people will think a bit and may say, "Family!"

I will reply, "That is good, but there is One higher than that" (or "more important than that"). And pointing up to the sky, I say, "And that is God!" If they still seem to be interested, I may say, "Do you know Jesus as your Savior?" I can tell by their answer whether they are saved or not. If they smile and answer in the affirmative, I know they are saved because 1 John:5:1 says, *"Whosoever believes that Jesus is the Christ is born of God; and everyone that loves him that begat, loves him that is begotten of Him."*

Of course, if they are unsaved and still interested, I will explain the plan of salvation briefly, so as not to lose their attention, perhaps using what is called the Roman Road, with such verses as Romans 3:23; 5:8, 6:23, and 10:9–13. Or if they seem to be busy or disinterested, I will leave them my little tract message, as below:

> Dear Friend, I may have spoken to you or I may have just left this note to tell or reiterate to you the most important thing in my life, which is: *Faith in Jesus Christ* as my Savior and Lord. I found Him [or rather, He found me] as a lonely, devastated teenager, weighing no more than one hundred pounds, facing my senior year in high school. To make it short, He gave me *peace, joy* and a *purpose* in this life, and Eternal Life in the hereafter [Rom 5:1, Gal. 5:22, John 3:16].
>
> I was on my way to Hell, as we all are, before coming to Him [Heb. 9:27] until I began reading the Bible, searching for an answer for my needy soul. I finally found that all of my trouble was that I, like all of us, was a guilty sinner before a Holy God [Rom. 3:23, Eccl. 1:2, Isa. 1:18]. But when I asked Jesus to come into my heart and forgive my sins, He did! And He will do the same for you, making your life *new* [2 Cor. 5:17]. And whatever your problem, you

can have this wonderful peace, joy, and a purpose in life [John 14:6].

What should you do? Confess to God that you are a sinner, and *repent* [Luke 13:3, 5] give up your sins and turn to God. Accept Jesus Christ as your Savior, Who suffered and died as the penalty for your sins and mine, and rose from the grave to prove that He is God. [Isa. 53:5, 6; Rom. 10:9–13]

If you have questions or want to know more, call me at 708-355-1654.

Richard

You might ask, why do you go out witnessing alone? Didn't Jesus send his disciples out in twos?

Yes, it is generally best to go out in twos so one can be praying while the other talks or to "intercept" and entertain small children who might interrupt the Gospel presentation, or to help in case of any threats of violence, etc. But who is willing to go with me? I don't even ask anyone because I know, unless they are "sold out" to the Lord, they do not want to go.

Of course, when Bettye was alive, we were a team, and we did go out together. My children tell me it is dangerous to go out alone, in these days, but I have never been in real danger in witnessing. Recently, a lady called the police as I offered her my "Gospel Tract." But I couldn't care less, except I felt sorry for the lady, who was fighting God and the Gospel. A little later, I saw two squad cars pull up.

I went right to the first car and said, "You are probably looking for me."

He replied, "What are you doing?"

I said, "I'm just talking to people about God." And I showed him one of my tracts.

He asked, "Are you selling anything?"

I answered, "No, not at all."

He said, "You are all right. You are not doing anything wrong." And he walked back to his squad car.

You ask, "Are you winning any souls?" Yes, but not a whole lot. Are people listening to me? Yes. Are Christians I meet, encouraged? Yes, I believe they are. They may be thinking, this is what we should be doing.

Am I sowing the seed of the Word of God? YES. Am I doing the will of God? YES, I believe I am, for Jesus said, "*The harvest truly is plenteous, but the laborers are few, pray therefore the Lord of the harvest, that He will send forth laborers into His harvest*" (Mat. 9:37, 38, KJV). Currently, I am taking four people to church, as a result of the above witnessing, one of them responding to the invitation to accept Christ as Savior, on his first time at the church.

THE CHICAGO MISSIONARY SOCIETY

I also worked for a little while for the Chicago Missionary Society, located on the Near North Side, under a Brother Nelson. They gave food to needy people and held services, also going door-to-door to help them. I also did some preaching there.

In going door-to-door, I found a place where they took in homeless young women and slept them on the floor. But men were also sleeping there, so it was suspicious that prostitution may also have been going on there. I reported it to Bro. Nelson. (I don't remember his full name), But nothing came of it, that I remember.

Bro. Nelson's wife was a Methodist Pentecostal—that is, she was one of those Methodists of old who sought desperately for John Wesley's doctrine of sanctification through "perfect love." She prayed in "tongues" and claimed she got it from travelling with her sister and brother-in-law, saying, "The Lord brought revival, 'Wherever He dropped us down!'"

RICHARD WESLEY LYTHBERG

PREACHING TO CROWDS IN DOWNTOWN CHICAGO

I used to preach in downtown Chicago. Once, a policeman stopped me, so I went down one block and continued preaching. The biggest crowd I preached to was on Wacker Drive, going to work in the morning or coming home at night. Once, on the latter scene, a man and a woman came over to talk to me. The man asked, "How long have you been on fire like this?" I didn't consider myself *on fire*, but a big crowd does inspire me. I was preaching rather fervently. I just told them I'm not always like this. But you see, we can encourage and inspire one another.

I don't know if I was breaking the law in preaching downtown. Possibly I was, because, years later, it was necessary to have a permit from the city government to preach downtown, which I obtained on a couple of occasions. Later, Bettye and I preached on the Lakefront, the beach on Lake Michigan. Again, a policeman stopped us; but this time, it was only because we were using an amplifier, a bullhorn. Why were we so intent on preaching? The Bible gives the answer: *"How shall they preach unless they are sent… How beautiful are the feet of those who preach the gospel of peace, who bring glad tidings of good things…faith comes by hearing, and hearing by the word of God"* (Rom. 10: 15, 17, NKJV).

"So shall My word be that goes forth from my mouth: it shall not return to my void, but it shall prosper in the thing for which I sent it" (Isa. 55:11, NKJV).

Later, after our marriage, Bettye and I would go on Sundays to Maxwell Street (a well-known Jewish area on Chicago's Near South Side, well-known for Polish and other kinds of hot dogs (and also, where Bettye received her home maternity care). We would preach there, and people would listen. Often, we would also use megaphones. And even tourists would take our pictures. It was just a novelty to them, apparently.

We got the idea from Bettye's sister, Eliza, who preached there. She would also take long rides on Greyhound buses, particularly to preach to the people on the buses. She would get permission from the bus drivers and even give "altar calls" or invitations to accept Christ as Savior.

I did not feel I should do as Eliza did, however, because then you are taking advantage of a "captive audience" and probably many did not want to listen to the Gospel. But again, the Spirit of God can cause people to listen, despite themselves. And I never did hear of anyone complaining about Eliza's preaching!

I did, however, give short testimonies or scriptural statements at Christian food pantries, where the authorities welcomed my testimonies and pleas for Christ.

My preaching on Pastor Matthew's Radio Program in Obuasi. (Joseph Annor in background)

School children, orphans, and teachers at Twifo Praso

Quadruplets in our Orphanage (Probably teenagers now)

Establishing a Church in village of Botodwina

My dear sweet children loved on me at the Village Crusade
Are they not sweet
(written by Bettye)

Bettye Ministering to Children in Ateiko
(Crusade in a Village)

Pastor Joshua Affori, His church
I preached week of revival meetings & we supported
Him, first in cape coast & then in Accra

Fire Festival (outdoor service to reach unchurched)

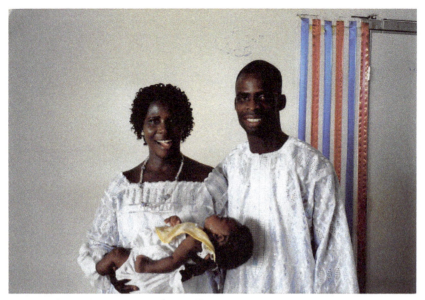

Patrick, preacher and "foreman" of School Building Project, and Felicia, our cook, and their baby

Our children in Twifo Praso, Ghana
Welcoming us (school & orphanage children)

Typical photo of a market in Ghana

Typical huts in a village in Ghana

Temporary school in Twifo Praso, the rain forest. The school started under pastor John Opoku, who was also s student in our original Bible School.

In 2000, Bettye went alone to Ghana and was very successful in crusade. She preached and celebrated her 64th birthday with Pastor & Mrs. Brister of the Assembly of God in Daboase.

Under Evangelist Joseph Annor
Children of our school in Bimbilla, in North Ghana, where there had been fighting between Christians & Muslims

Bible school graduation, Pastor Matthew's School

Ghanians love to dance & praise the lord, Pastor Mathew's church meeting in a school. He later built 2 churches & even had a Bible School in So. Africa.

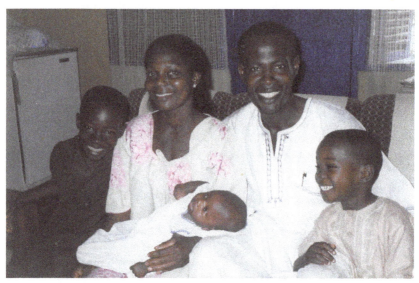

Pastor Matthew Kwesi & Family, student in our Bible School & after led his Bible School & church in Obuasi, the Gold Mine city.

Linda Morgan asked if she could stay with us in Takoradi, when we first went to Ghana to start a Bible School.
I think she stayed for 2 or more weeks, praying for a husband. We met her again, years later, when we heard her husband preaching & found they had a church in Accra, the Capitol City. She is holding baby, her husband on extreme right from her. Unfortunately he died from a dog bite after we left Ghana. Others incl. her mother & children. Now has 5 children.

Deeda Priscilla was only 4 yrs. old when her father wanted to sell her, but her mother brought her to our orphanage instead. It was difficult to get her to smile in those days. Here she is as a young teenager!

Street meeting in Kenya, with Djaguna
(Went there first in 1993, a 5-week trip)

While in Africa, Bettye loved and missed her grandchildren, Jaylenn and Jacen, now 15 and 17 years old, Rebecca's children.

Our children
Rebecca, age 17 and David, age 19.

Rebecca went with us on our first trip to Takoradi, Ghana

Our family, before going to Africa (1980's)

Our first child, Mary, with Roman, now a master's degree student and his sister, now a nurse.

Bettye and I, visiting a prisoner in a Southern Illinois prison.

"Mickey" with her husband and five children, which would not have been possible if Bettye had taken the abortion pill. All their children are "grown up" now and they have 2 grandchildren.

Wedding, Dec. 23, 1969

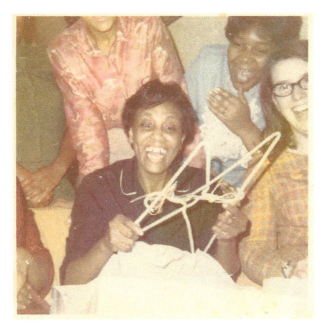

Bettye at her wedding shower

Bettye, H.S. Grad
Shaw, Mississipi

Childhood Bettye with younger brother,
Bynum (Ben), ages unknown

CHAPTER 7

THE MIRACULOUS BAPTISM OF THE HOLY SPIRIT

Did not our hearts burn within us?
—Luke 24:32

I can still see him in my mind's eye, a young African American man, unclothed from the waist up, grimacing in pain and begging me to pray for his urgent abdominal condition. I did so, the best I could, but somehow sensed that we had not prayed victoriously. I was at the notorious Cook County Hospital on Chicago's Near West Side, where poor people went for all their medical needs, simply because the prices were lower than anywhere else.

But you may have to wait several hours for service, as I had, once for myself, and once for a nephew, with terrible strep throat pains. I was twenty-two years of age at the time and was just beginning to be serious about my spiritual condition. I was there at the hospital with my cousin, Shirley Wachholz, who was an assistant to Chaplain Lilly, a well-known black servant minister who would cut hair, trim toenails, and help the patients in any way he could.

Shirley, whom I respected greatly, said to me, "You take the men's wards," as she proceeded into the women's wards to pray for the needy people. (That was all the instruction she gave me.)

When we met again at closing time for visitors, I saw Chaplain Lilly standing by the doors, as a big crowd of people were leaving the hospital. The visitors were taking gospel tracts out of a big supply in the ample hands of the counselor. It was a sight to behold! Lilly was making no attempt to pass the tracts out. They were just greedily taking them out of his hands! That is how well respected he was.

As my cousin drove me home, I told her how I didn't know how to pray for the poor young black man, who so desperately wanted me to pray for him. She said to me, "*That is because you haven't been filled with the Holy Spirit.*"

I believed her and began to set this quest for the Baptism of the Holy Spirit, as the greatest need in my life.

I knew that Shirley had been a bit rebellious as a teenager, smoking cigarettes for a while. But I also knew that she had a terrible skin disease (eczema) that covered her from head to toe. But she also had one great desire in life, and that was to be a school teacher (like our aunt Hilma).

But she knew that the Board of Education would never accept her with a skin disease. Somehow, she began attending a Nazarene church, which believed in the healing ministry of Jesus Christ. And lo and behold, she was healed (from head to toe)!

Later she was certified by the Chicago Board of Education (now known as the Chicago Public Schools) and became an excellent teacher, being named teacher of the year once. I know she loved her pupils, prayed for them, and witnessed to them, when appropriate.

HOW SHIRLEY RECEIVED THE BAPTISM OF THE HOLY SPIRIT

Later, Shirley married Ed Lombard, a TV cameraman for WLS, channel 7, and a solid Christian. They began attending Beulah Temple, a Pentecostal Church, near 75th and Cottage Grove on the South Side. (Incidentally, the pastor's daughter there later became the director of the Gospel Tabernacle Choir, a famous singing group in New York City.)

I think my cousin snickered a little at these Full Gospel people at first, like most of us did, but Ed told her not to make fun of them, as they are God's people. And she took it to heart.

Shirley was a singer and often sang solos. I used to love to hear her sing because she had a strong forceful voice. One of the songs I loved to hear her sing went something like this—"How well do I remember, as I doubted day by day, for I did not know for certain, that my sins were washed away. But it's *real,* it's *real,* praise God, my doubts are settled, for I know, I know it's *real!*"

But once they called Shirley to come up on the platform and sing a solo, and when she walked up and opened her mouth to sing, no words came out. She could not sing! She was embarrassed, humiliated, mortified, as she had to walk down, a failure!

I don't know the reason for this failure, but God has a way of humbling us, showing us, that, after all, we are all *nothing*, zero, without Him! She told me she went to the lakefront the next day, Monday, just to pray and meditate concerning what had happened to her. I don't know if it was there at Lake Michigan, or soon after, but I know she was filled to overflowing, with the Holy Spirit (and she spoke with other tongues, as the Spirit gave her utterance, just like the apostles, on the Day of Pentecost. See Acts 2:4, KJV).

Shirley became a bold witness to anyone who would listen to her about salvation from our sins, through the atonement of Jesus Christ on the cross and the Baptism of the Holy Spirit. She had three daughters. It was probably the first one that she used to carry in her arms to keep her from crying, while she preached and walked up and down in the Salvation Army Chapel.

I was about to start at Wheaton College and considered not going because I felt that nothing was more important than receiving the Baptism of the Holy Spirit.

But I did go to Wheaton, and surely, God was leading. Somehow, I found out that some students who believed in the Baptism of the Holy Spirit had a prayer meeting every day at 5 p.m. Dick Shrout, probably my best friend at Wheaton, seemed to be the leader. At least, he was always there. One weekend, I went home with him to Decatur, Illinois. Dick had received the Baptism, but was still a Conservative Baptist and took me to his church. But he also took me to see his friend, who was a Pentecostal Pastor. I was very interested in what he had to say. Little did I know it would be more than ten years before I would receive the great infilling!

The Bible says, in Luke 24:32, that after the death (and resurrection of Jesus) two of the disciples were going to Emmaus, and Jesus appeared and walked with them. But they did not recognize Him. However, when they invited him to stay overnight with them, suddenly their eyes were opened, seeing the nail holes in His wrists, and He vanished out of their sight. Then they said, "Did not our hearts burn within us, while He opened the Word to us, on the way?"

That is how I felt, much of the time, as I sought for this experience—my heart burned like fire. I was motivated, as I read about it, prayed and fasted, walked up and down in the Forest Preserve near my house, as I went to many churches and meetings, praying, and having others pray for me that I might *receive*.

But I did *not* receive. But that did not dampen my spirit. I kept on seeking, talking to people about it. Some told me "God has a time for you. Don't be discouraged." Some say, "Well. You didn't know how to yield your tongue to God." That may be have been true, but when I did receive the Baptism, it was with such power, that it seemed I could not resist.

HOW I RECEIVED THE BAPTISM OF THE HOLY SPIRIT

It was while I was pastoring the Bethany Baptist Church in Chicago. I was reading a book by T. L. and Daisy Osborne, called *Bible Days Are Here Again*, telling about the miracles resulting from the Baptism of the Spirit. I also read the *Christian Life* magazine, which had been an evangelical periodical, until the editor, himself, received the Baptism. Now they were writing about miracles happening in the lives of denominational ministers, through the Holy Spirit. I was particularly interested in the work of Dennis Bennett, an Episcopalian Priest, who was having so many miraculous healings in Van Nuys, California, that he was sent to Seattle, Washington, apparently because the healings embarrassed the church leadership. *But* the miracles continued in the north, just as they had in the south!

When I called the editor, Bob Walker, to find out about Dennis Bennett, he invited me to come and see him. I did and he told me how wonderful it was for him now to *worship* in spirit and truth! But instead of giving me Bennett's address, he suggested that I visit the Trinity Episcopal Church in Wheaton for a prayer meeting in the afternoon. Though I didn't know it, God was leading all the way!

Since I had lived in the city of Wheaton, while going to school there, I had an idea where Trinity was and found it handily. I was impressed by the man wearing a clerical collar and praying, "Thank you, Father," for answered prayer and the like. I thought this was wonderful, but not what I was expecting, so I decided it was time for me to leave.

But I had seen in the audience a man whom I knew, as a student at Wheaton. He was then a grad student, who occasionally attended our prayer meeting. His name was Bill Menzies, but he had already left the prayer meeting.

Since this was about nine years since I had left Wheaton, I thought it quite a coincidence that he was there the same time as I was there. So I decided to go to the old Tower Building before I went home to see if I could find out if Menzies was perhaps a teacher at Wheaton now. Bill, who was a rather quiet fellow, had told me years before that he had been a Presbyterian, but having heard of the Pentecostal Experience, he decided to attend the school of the Assemblies of God denomination, in Springfield, Missouri, to see if there really was anything to this Baptism of the Holy Spirit. So he began to seek for it, until one night, he received and was so "drunk in the Spirit" that they had to carry him home! (See Ephesians 5:18.) Menzies later became very prominent as an editor of the Full Gospel Bible.

However, it was now evening and the offices where I was going to inquire were already closed. But there still were some students there, so I thought I would ask one of them if he knew whether Menzies was teaching at Wheaton. I saw a couple of fellows and was about to ask them, but they appeared to be preoccupied in conversation, so I decided to ask the fellow right behind them.

So I said, "Say, do you happen to know if you have a teacher here named Bill Menzies?"

The fellow, who turned out to be grad student named Tim Jessen, replied, "What do you know about Bill Menzies?"

I told him I had known him as a student at Wheaton some years before.

This fellow, whom, of course, I had never seen before, asked me, "Are you interested in the Charismatic Revival?"

I answered, "Yes, as a matter of fact, I am." (This is what I had been reading about in the *Christian Life* and other magazines.)

He then "floored" me with the question, "Do you want the Baptism of the Holy Spirit?"

I replied again, as before, "Yes, as a matter of fact, I do."

Tim asked, "You were at the Episcopal Church and left?" (I had told him that I had seen Menzies there.)

"Come on back!" he said. "*You have an appointment with God!*"

We went back to a formal evening service, with the priest wearing a robe and genuflections by the congregation, reminding me of nothing but a Catholic church! Toward the end of the service, those who wanted prayer were asked to come forward. Tim asked me if I wanted to do so. Of course, I did!

Then this Baptist pastor (me) came forward and knelt before an Episcopal priest, whom I thought before was only "half-saved" and asked him to pray that I might receive the Baptism of the holy Spirit. This, I believe, was the purpose of it all. That we must "*Humble [our] selves under the mighty hand of God, that He may exalt [us] in due time*" (1 Peter 5:6, KJV).

Again, the words of peter to Cornelius' household was about to be fulfilled in my life. "*In truth I perceive that God shows no partiality. But in every nation whoever fears Him and works righteousness is accepted by Him*" (Acts 10:34b, 35, NKJV).

The service ended then, with nothing extraordinary occurring, but I was told there would be refreshments downstairs and another informal service. At this point, Tim had to leave, and I have not seen him again until this day, but we have talked recently by telephone because of what was about to happen to me, at that time.

During the time of refreshments, I saw a lady whom I met at Faith Tabernacle on the North Side, whose husband was a seminary professor at Winona Lake, Indiana. She knew what I was there for and looked at me with pleading eyes, saying, "You will never be good enough. Just reach out to God by faith, and He will bless you." There was also a lady there whom I used to hear, singing on WMBI, the Moody Bible Institute radio station.

Finally, the informal meeting began with the singing of choruses. It seemed to me that there was a very good spirit of love present as people began giving messages in tongues (unknown languages) and then, the interpretations. There were three in all. Again, anyone who wanted prayer was asked to come up. I was the second one who came for prayer. They seated me in a chair and several laid hands on me, as they began to pray, the priest taking the lead. I heard him pray, "Inasmuch as he is a preacher of Your Word." And my heart said, "Oh, yes, lord, that is why I want Your Spirit!"

Suddenly, I felt a great power coming upon me. I took three deep breaths. (I don't know why, except for the Father, the Son, and the Holy Spirit.) Then, I felt a great infusion of power upon me and jumped to my feet, but they pulled me back to my seat. (They apparently don't do such things in the Episcopal Church.) Again, this happened three times. Later, I also attributed that to the Trinity, as that *was* the name of the church!

My tongue was flip-flopping around in my mouth as I began to speak in "tongues." Someone remarked it was maybe a Zulu tongue, as they make "clicks." But no, I just did not know how to fully yield my tongue to the Lord.

My first thought, after this experience was that this is more of the same Spirit that I already knew. And this is borne out by the Scriptures. Jesus breathed on his disciples and said, *"Receive the Holy Spirit"* (John 20:22 [before His atonement]). I believe this is the most underrated verse of the Bible. The apostles were baptized into the Holy Spirit on the Day of Pentecost (Acts 2:4). As I say, this bears out the thought that it *is* a "second" work of grace.

Also, that it is not true that one must speak in other tongues to be saved. Romans 8:9 says, "If any man has not the Spirit of Christ, he is none of His," showing that although the disciples may have already been born again (since the Holy Spirit had not yet been given), but it is analogous of the new birth, which is now received at conversion, as every "born again" Christian (John 3:1–7) has the Spirit of Christ. John 1:12 states that *"as many as received Him, to them gave He the power to become the sons (or children) Of God."*

But I had a lot to learn. Some of us think that once we have received the baptism of the Holy Spirit, we have "arrived." But that is not true! Now that you have the power of the Spirit, you have just begun! It is like another new birth.

I, myself, with "all my education, etc.," did not understand, because I reasoned, if I am filled with the Holy Spirit, there is no more room for sin, I am perfect. Of course, it didn't take very long for me to see I was yet far from perfect. What I had to learn was that although there *is* one baptism, there are *many* fillings. We do not always walk around full of the spirit, but we have that potential, and the spirit can come upon us at any time, if we are open to Him.

However, to sum up my experience, *I did receive the baptism of the Holy Spirit! It was miraculous* and beyond dispute that it was a work of God!

1. Consider the possibility of it being a mere coincidence that Bill Menzies and I should happen to be in the same prayer meeting, in the same church, with which, neither one of us had anything to do.

2. We were there at the very same time, *nine* years after we were both students at Wheaton College at the same time.
3. Even though the above was true, I had no idea why he was there, and if I had interrupted the conversation and asked the first two students about Menzies, they undoubtedly would have known nothing about him being there (doing research concerning the Charismatic Revival) and I would have gone home unfulfilled and disappointed.
4. *But God...thank God!* He had me wait and ask the man behind the others! What are the chances that probably the only one in the school would happen to be there at that moment, who could speak to me as he did, and tell me that I had *an appointment with God*, and though he did not see the fulfillment, he, as it were, "laid hands on me," spiritually and brought me back to the church, so "foreign" to both of us, but where I received the Spiritual fulfillment I had sought, for over ten years! *Praise God!*

Although this happened more than fifty years ago, I am just beginning to realize what a miracle it was! How God loved me all those, almost eleven, years. I was seeking, fasting, praying, and then, the *miracle* happened. I'm almost glad it took so long because that made me appreciate, more so, what God had done for me! How He loves me, and how He loves *you*, whoever is reading this! He loves us! Never doubt it! Continue to trust Him and praise Him, and he will bring you out to the place He wants you to be!

HOW BETTYE RECEIVED THE BAPTISM OF THE HOLY SPIRIT

In direct contrast to me, and most others, my wife, Bettye (before we were married or even acquainted), without spending *any* time to speak of, in seeking, received the great baptism of the Holy Spirit.

Here is how it happened. Although she lived on the West Side, I believe she met some of the young people of the Evangelical Christian Church on the South Side (which was actually a Pentecostal church), through a summer camp. Paul Evans, a man of God, who later became our pastor, invited her to a revival meeting.

Bettye, who was already a student at the Moody Bible Institute, loved the Lord and wanted to be filled with the Spirit, according to Ephesians 5:18: *"Be not drunk with wine, wherein is excess, but be filled with the Spirit."* But she did not want to act like some of the Pentecostal people. So when offering time came, she let Bro. Evans take her offering up front, because the custom was to shake the pastor's hand.

But on the second night of the revival, Paul refused to take her offering up, saying, "Take it up, yourself." So she did, *but she never got back to her seat!* When the pastor shook her hand, the power of God knocked her off her feet. And she laid there all during the service, prophesying to the people and to herself, uncovering her pride, that she had judged the people, when she herself was guilty. After the service, they were turning off the lights, but Bettye was still lying on the floor, prophesying. Bro. Evans was afraid they would miss the last bus back to the West Side, if they didn't pick her up!

You say, "How do you know that she received the Baptism of the Holy Spirit, if she did not speak in tongues?" Because, like Saul of Tarsus (Paul, the apostle), ever after he received, she also spoke in "tongues," ever after that experience. And no doubt, she did so along with the prophesying, that night.

The Bible is the Rule Book and the Manual for anyone who really wants to live right, live for God, and be right with God. As a student in a Baptist Seminary and as a Baptist pastor, I was taught that the New Testament was what we followed for doctrine and practice.

The New Testament, in the book of the Acts of the Apostles, explains five events where people were baptized or filled with the Holy Spirit. (The apostles and others in Acts, chapter two;

the Samaritans, in Acts 8, Saul, who became Paul, in Acts 9, Cornelius' household, chapters 10 and 11, and the disciples of John the Baptist at Corinth, chapter 19. In three cases, Scripture states, "They spoke in tongues.")

In Acts 8, concerning the "revival" led by Phillip, Peter and John came to pray that the new converts would receive the Holy Spirit. They did and the magician, Simon, *witnessed something he wrongly coveted*—the ability to lay hands on people to receive the Baptism of the Holy Spirit. What he witnessed was undoubtedly the speaking in "tongues" of the converts that caused him to want this gift (as if it was magic, as he had been a magician [Acts 8:14–19, KJV]).

In the case of Paul, he says later, "I speak in tongues more than all of you" (1 Cor. 14:18, KJV). When did Paul begin to "speak in tongues?" We can safely infer that it was when he was baptized with the holy Spirit (Acts 9:17–22, KJV)

Therefore, according to the Bible, the *initial evidence* of the Baptism of the Holy Spirit is the miraculous speaking in *other* tongues, that is, in a language that is not known by the speaker. There are many cases of people hearing their own language spoken by a person who did not know their language.

Many years ago, now, in a church in Los Angeles, that I attended, a man gave a message in tongues. We learned later, that a man from Italy was present, who said the message was in perfect Italian. Just a few days ago, as I write, Evangelist Jimmy Swaggart told of being in Africa, hearing a man speaking English, among the nationals who did not know English. He said, "I didn't know you knew English." His words had to be interpreted to the man because he did *not* know English! He was speaking in tongues, in English, telling about the Gospel in various books of the New Testament! Also, some years ago, I spoke to a pastor who told me he once preached a whole sermon in "tongues" to his congregation. He was speaking in Polish! There was a man present from Poland, who heard and understood the sermon in Polish!

However, today, many do not believe in, or do not experience or recognize the *"power from on high"* (Luke 24:49) that

Jesus told his disciples was necessary for them to be effective witnesses of the Gospel (Good News) that *Jesus died for the sins of the whole world* so that everyone who believed and trusted in Him as their personal Savior from sin and its punishment, hell, would be saved and have Eternal Life! "*You shall receive power when the Holy Spirit has come upon you; and you shall be witnesses to Me in Jerusalem, and in all Judea and Samaria, and to the end of the earth*" (Acts 1:8, NKJV).

Because they have not received or believed in the great infilling of the Holy Spirit, many evangelical preachers and theologians have argued that the experience is not for today and was only needed to get the new church started in the first century.

They have turned to the thirteenth chapter of 1 Corinthians, verse 10, where we read, "*When that which is perfect is come, than that which is in part shall be done away.*" So the theologians say that the newly formed church, in the first century did not yet have the full *Bible* (the Word of God)—that is the "*perfect*" or "*mature*" that was needed. We no longer need a "push" to start the *church*, they say. We no longer need miracles of healing, speaking in tongues, and casting out of demons, as depicted in the sixteenth chapter of Mark.

I say, NO. The *perfect* is *not* the Bible, but "*The Lord Jesus Christ, Himself,*" Who is yet to come! When He comes, He will destroy all the enemies of the Church and of *Israel*, the chosen People of God, when they march against them. And Jesus will finally *return*! He shall set His feet on the Mt. of Olives. (See chapters 18–22 of the book of the Revelation.)

But let us look at the world today. If you look at a world map or globe, you will see that none of the nations are truly Christian nations. Even our great nation is no longer a Christian nation, if it ever was. Yes, there used to be prayer in our schools, postings of the Ten Commandments, Bible reading, etc. Our greatest universities, such as Yale, Harvard, and Princeton, were started as schools to educate preachers!

The much-cited "Separation of Church and State" was not affirmed to keep God out of politics but to avoid any church or denomination from becoming a state or national religion. But the United States and Great Britain (United Kingdom) were greatly used by God to spread the Word by missionaries. They were successful in bringing Jesus Christ and the Gospel of Eternal Life to Africa, India, South America, and parts of Asia.

But many nations, not only restrict the Gospel but disallow and restrict Christians. I'm speaking of all Moslem countries, as well as Communistic countries, particularly China. Although we are told that there are at least one hundred million of Christians in China, there are no true Christian churches in which they can worship and avoid persecution, prison sentences, and even death. So they must worship in forbidden house churches.

Therefore, when we look at the world with wars; racism; terrorism; with nations, including our own, accepting homosexual marriage, in direct contradiction of the Word of God; and other nations officially outlawing or resisting the Gospel of Jesus Christ, the only way of salvation from sin, how then can we say that the power of the Holy Spirit is no longer needed, and the Bible is enough?

It is true that the Bible is the only hope for the world, not the Koran, or any Hindu or Buddhist texts, or other books, can bring salvation to the needy souls of mankind! No book compares to the Bible, which means "library"! Sixty-six books, written over a span of 1,500 years, by forty writers, all inspired by the Holy Spirit of God. *"No prophecy of the Scripture is of any private interpretation. For the prophecy came not in old time by the will of man, but holy men of God spake as they were moved by the Holy Ghost"* (2 Peter 1:20, 21, KJV).

From Genesis 3:15, the prophecy that the seed of the woman (Mary, the only woman who ever carried a seed), given by the Holy Spirit (Luke 1:31, 35) would bruise the head of (and defeat Satan) and bring Eternal Life to all who believed, is the story of the Bible, told by forty authors, culminating in the return of Christ to earth in victory over every foe and the New Jerusalem coming down from heaven.

The Bible is the only book which, if followed, can heal the brokenhearted; give courage to the fainthearted; heal the sick; bring deliverance from liquor and drug addiction, sex addiction, or any other malady!

But the Word of God can only adequately do these things if proclaimed and anointed by Holy Spirit-filled believers. Therefore, seeing that the need and condition of the world is as great as it was in the first century, the baptism of the Holy Spirit is as much needed today as it was on the day of Pentecost!

"THE STORY OF THREE MEN"

Sometime after Bettye and I were married, we had some charges against our pastor, who was a white man, but most of the congregation were African Americans. I won't mention the charges, except to say that, years later, they have been substantiated.

Meanwhile, we joined Progressive Beulah Pentecostal Church (a union of two different churches). I became the Sunday school superintendent for a while, and occasionally preached there. A wise old gray-headed lady used to talk about the story of "three men." I never heard her tell the story, but since I knew who the three men were, I believe I can tell about them.

The first man was *William Seymour*, the son of former slaves. It was said that he had spiritual experiences, night dreams and visions as a youth. (Hyatt, Eddie, *The Azusa Street Revival, The Holy Spirit in America, 100 Years*, Special Centennial Edition, by TBN, Charisma House, A Strang Company, 600 Rhinehart Road, Lake Mary, Fl. 2746, 2006, page 23).

He lost an eye to smallpox but said that for two and one-half years, he prayed five hours a day (Ibid.). He was hungry for God, seeking the Baptism of the Holy Spirit, when he met Charles Parham in Houston, Texas. Parham's Bible school in Topeka, Kansas, had begun receiving the Baptism on New Year's Eve 1900, with several experiencing it soon after. Parham was preaching and teaching about the Pentecostal experience in 1906, but because of segregation laws, Parham could not let him in the classroom. So with the door open, he sat outside the room to hear the teaching!

Although Seymour was pastoring a church in Houston, he was then called to pastor a church in Los Angeles, California. Believing this was God's will, he went to L.A. and began to preach about the great Holy Spirit infilling, although he had not yet experienced it, personally!

The church had embraced John Wesley's doctrine of sanctification, which they called the Baptism of the Holy Spirit, but they rejected the speaking in tongues, as Seymour preached it, calling it false doctrine! *After his first sermon as pastor*, he was locked out when he came for the evening service! (Ibid. p. 27).

Although the officials of the church had rejected Seymour's message, some were still zealously interested, so they began meeting in a home, and soon, so many received the Baptism of the Holy Spirit, with speaking in tongues, that they were overcrowded, and needed more room.

So, they rented a former stable on Azusa St., and after a thorough cleaning, began services. And soon crowds of people began filling the new meeting place. Even newspaper reporters and other skeptics came and were converted.

Little did Seymour know that he would soon be leading a movement, largely, by putting his head in a box, to pray (a box which they used for a pulpit), a movement that would continue day and night, for three years, that would spring several Pentecostal denominations into being, would send missionaries throughout the world, would bring physical healing to many, would cast out demons, and would be said to be responsible for six hundred million followers. It was the beginning of the world-wide Pentecostal Revival.

We learn some lessons from the life of William Seymour. (1) That it was a humble black man, who undoubtedly did not have the education of many of the white men who came to receive the Baptism of the Spirit that he preached and brought to the mission on Azusa Street, even though he had not yet experienced it! But *he had a great hunger for God!*

(2) That the Azusa Street Revival was a "black thing," in that it began among "colored people," as they were called then. Since they were locked out of their church, Seymour and a few sympathizers, went to a home to hold a prayer service, and the Holy Spirit fell upon them, and several began to "speak in tongues!" It started with Lucy Farrow, the niece of Frederick Douglas, laying her hands on a brother, seeking the "baptism." It was said of her that anyone she laid hands on received the "blessing." But when he asked, she said, "I cannot do it, unless the Lord tells me to do it." But later, she said the Lord told her to lay hands on him. And she did. And he did! (He began speaking in tongues.) Later, when others arrived for their meeting, he raised his hands and began speaking in tongues. Several others received "their baptisms," also speaking in tongues. Soon, the home was too small for the crowds that were coming. That was when they moved to Azusa Street, and people came from all over, when they heard that God was pouring out His Spirit "on all flesh" (Acts 2:17a, NKJV).

(3) As we said, the meetings went on at Azusa Street, night and day, for three years! They went on till late at night and started again at midmorning. People of all races came! And I believe the white people were blessed because *they were willing to join with African Americans!* Therefore, they shared in the same blessings from God! There is a photo of John G. Lake and other white leaders with Bro. Seymour. Lake later had a great healing career in South Africa and tells of his church of twenty thousand people being blessed by Seymour's preaching (Hyatt, p. 33).

A man named G. B. Cashwell came from North Carolina, when he read about the Azusa Street outpouring. But when an African American man laid hands on him to pray for his baptism, he left the meeting, offended! But God got a hold of him and he repented! He went back to Azusa Street and asked Seymour and other blacks to pray for him. He testified that he, then, spoke in "tongues," several languages! Seymour took an offering for him to return to North Carolina. He did so and rented a building for a monthlong revival meeting, which went on in the east, among the Pentecostal Holiness churches (Ibid, p. 38).

The other two men were Charles Prince Jones and Charles Mason. They were Baptists seeking a deeper life and were said to have accepted the Wesleyan doctrine of sanctification, also. But when Mason learned of the revival in California, he went there and stayed five weeks, saying he was gloriously filled with the Spirit. But when he returned, after much debate, Jones would not accept the Baptism with the speaking in tongues. They had called their church, *the Church of God in Christ* (Ibid, p. 40).

Mason kept the name, but Jones, a great songwriter (who was my wife's pastor in her growing up, in Mississippi), said "speaking in tongues is scriptural, but not necessary." He took the name of "the Church of Christ Holiness" for him and his followers. I must say that there are several churches still following his teaching. But Mason's church is now the largest Pentecostal denomination in our country with about 5,500,000 followers (op cit.).

Today, many Pentecostal churches no longer stress the Baptism of the Holy Spirit! We have lost our distinction, our specialty! Not only Pentecostal, but Evangelical churches, as well, have lost the *fire*! And the only way to regain that "fire" is to seek the Lord, become hungry again, like William Seymour! Like Jesse Jackson's Rainbow Coalition emphasis of some time ago, PUSH—*Pray until something happens!*

CHAPTER 8

BETTYE!

I kid you not, it was not love at first sight!

A WHITE MAN IN A BLACK WORLD

After I received the great infilling of the Holy Spirit (miraculously) at the Trinity Episcopal Church in Wheaton, Illinois, on April 25, 1963, I was invited (by one of those who had laid hands on me and prayed) to the meetings of the Full Gospel Business Men's Fellowship, led by Demos Shakarian.

After attending a few of the meetings, I was invited to a luncheon held by the FGBMFI. As God would have it, a certain man (whom I will not name) came late and sat at the same table as I. He was introduced and got up to make an announcement and prayer request for the school he operated in the inner-city area on the South Side.

I talked with him after the luncheon and told him (a white man) that I was interested in the school (which was about 95 percent African American). At that point, I did not remember how God had put it on my heart to help those people on the South Side, whom I saw as a teenager, riding the "EL" (Elevated train).

He surprised me by asking me if I wanted to be the manager of the school. I did not feel qualified, neither was I interested in being manager. But I told him I would not mind being a teacher of the school. So he hired me, and I started that fall, teaching seventh and eighth grades.

One of my eighth-grade pupils was Annie Baker. She was a good student but had some problems with arithmetic. The school held monthly parent-teacher conferences. At one of those conferences, I spoke to Annie's mother, Bettye Baker, about Annie's difficulty with math. I said, "Don't be too hard on her, she is doing the best she can." But Annie told her later, that she was *not* doing the best she could. So it seemed that I was not doing my job as her teacher!

I heard more from Bettye Baker on the day of the Big Snow in 1967! Since it was snowing steadily, the students were released one hour earlier, at 2 p.m. We had nineteen inches of snow that day! And some more the next day. As it turned out, many people, including my brother, Bill, could not get home and had to stay downtown, overnight!

Bettye kept calling me on the phone, asking me where her daughter was. All I could say was that we had dismissed the pupils early and the traffic was slow. It seemed as if she was blaming me or the school for her being late. Finally, she got home at eight p.m. (But they lived on the West Side, so she had to go quite a few miles.)

The next time I had a "run in" with Bettye Baker was on *Parents Day*, as we were preparing for eighth-grade graduation. Somehow, Bettye told me how she went to Harlem, New York, as a home missionary, and that she wanted to be a foreign missionary. But because it was so hard for her in Harlem, the Lord had shown her that she must marry before going to the foreign field. (Incidentally, we both wanted to go to India, as missionaries.)

But my reaction was, "Why is she telling me all this? I hardly know her." I said, in my heart, "I hope she is not thinking of me as a husband." And, truly she was not, at that time.

However, here is how it all changed. Bettye was a youth worker in our church, conducting the Young Peoples' Services, with Ed Taylor, assistant pastor and organist. The youth services were in the model of the adult services, with prophecy and prayer included. (Bettye also sang solos, as she had a very good singing voice.)

But there was no "love affair" going on between us, until the youth group was invited to a youth conference in St. Paul, Minnesota, and Ed invited me to come along. Somehow, I felt that God wanted me to go. I was then in my late thirties. But it had nothing to do with Bettye, or so I thought. I felt it was God's will because I knew some of the young people.

We took a train to St. Paul, leaving at nighttime. One of the young men asked Bettye to change seats with him, as he wanted to be with his friends. She did and found herself sitting right across from **me**! She said later that she thought I was boring, so she closed the door on me, as we had sleeping berths. She wrote in one of her books later that the Lord convicted her of being rude to me, so she opened the door again, and we seemed to have a good conversation.

During the conference, it just seemed natural for us to sit together. The "young people" were not children. They were teenagers, but not wild. They did not need overseeing, and of course, the local people were conducting the meetings. Anyway, this was the beginning of our chaotic courting.

Just a year or two before, I was about to marry a white girl. I took her to a jewelry store to see what kind of ring she would like for an engagement ring. And that was the last time I saw her!

At any rate, I am not proud of what I did. But I had *no peace,* after going to the jewelry store. It had nothing to do with the potential price of the ring. My brother, Bill, even came to see me and tried to comfort me, perhaps when he heard I was making paper balls and throwing them against the wall.

I was involved as an evangelist with the Assemblies of God at the time and went to Wisconsin to preach for one day, Sunday only. When I arrived at the pastor's home, it was filled with peace, in direct contrast to my troubled heart. The pastor had just resigned from his church and did not know what he was going to do next, but he had *peace.*

You might ask, "How could you preach, without *peace*?" After Bettye and I were married, when I was scheduled to preach, I put everything else out of my mind, even when she felt there was something wrong between us and couldn't understand how I could do it. But preaching was the most important thing in my life, and I would let nothing come between me and God, not even my wife. So I preached twice that Sunday, but I have no remembrance of what I said. I drove home late Sunday night (with no peace).

Early the next morning, I called the young lady and told her I had no peace. She said, "I'm through." I took her at her word! But I should have seen her face-to-face. Yet I had nothing I could say to her! *God would not let me marry her.* I did not know why at the time. Later, after Bettye and I were married, my mother told me that my former almost-fiancée said she had forgiven me for "jilting" her. I wrote her, saying that I did not call myself jilting her, but I did apologize for not seeing her, face-to-face. I left no return address on my letter because I wanted no possible interference to my marriage with Bettye. Strangely enough, it was not until I wrote these words, fifty years later, that I realized I could **not** marry the young lady, because God wanted me to marry Bettye, although I had not even met her, or knew that she existed, at that time!

Back to Bettye. We attended the same church, affiliated with the school, and I taught a Sunday school class, including some of my school pupils, particularly Annie. One Sunday, after the class, I saw Bettye standing with Annie, and if God ever spoke to me, He spoke to me then (in my spirit), saying, *"There is your wife and daughter."*

We had just a few "dates." I think the first one was at the Prudential Building. At that time, it was the highest building in Chicago. I can't remember how many floors it was, but we were on the highest floor for dinner. Bettye was just getting over a "cold" and could hardly eat. She also had trouble with her esophagus (which incidentally, also bothered her after we were married, at times, particularly in Africa). She had trouble eating and keeping the food down. I felt very sorry for her.

I think our next date was at a North Side church where some Korean children were singing. I remember saying something about being willing to marry her, if it was God's will, even if my parents were against it. This bothered Bettye, somewhat.

Unbeknownst to me, Bettye had been praying with a lady friend about a husband for her. About this time, she said to her, "Hey, God sent me a man, but he is a *white man!*" Her prayer partner countered, "We didn't specify any color!" (In other words, you better take what God gives you!)

I think we went to the Moody Bible Institute, where Bettye had been a student, on one date, but I can't remember the program. We also went to a zoo, on the Near North Side. One date I remember very vividly. Although Bettye lived on the West Side, with her Godmother, Sister Cokes, for some reason she was on the South Side, where I picked her up. It was a picnic, but we were late. In fact, we never found the picnic! When we arrived, we heard talk about a "race riot" or racial fighting. That did not make us feel very good, being an interracial couple! We might be in danger. But thank God, it was about over, when we got there. And we could not find the people from our church who were supposed to be there! So it was frustrating—illustrating why I called our courting chaotic!

And our troubles were not yet over! We both got involved in volunteer work with Prevention Inc., an organization like Teen Challenge, working with drug addicts. We stayed in the home permanently, helping the addicts, going through withdrawal, with Bible reading, prayer, back massages, whatever it took. And Bettye and I were getting very close.

However, one morning, Bettye had gone somewhere, I don't remember where. But I had my morning devotions and read Romans 14:21 where Paul says, *"It is good neither to eat flesh, nor drink wine, nor anything whereby thy brother stumbleth, or is offended, or is made weak"* (KJV).

I applied this Scripture to Bettye and I, concerning my parents who disapproved of my plans to marry her. Although I knew that their attitude was racist and prejudiced, I was deeply convicted that I was hurting, not my brother, but my parents.

I feared God and felt I had to get out of that environment of Prevention Inc. *I fled*. It was not pretty. I confess it now as I state in the title of this memoir, these are my confessions. I left a note for Bettye, I believe, but it was so long ago, I don't remember what I said. I was literally scared of God. It was very immature of me and hard to reconcile it with the fact that at the end, I was very sure that it was God's will for us to marry, despite my parents' reaction.

But I missed her greatly, could not forget her, thought about her constantly! I went back to school, taking education classes at Loyola University on the West Side, preparing, hopefully, to get a teaching certificate. But being in an African American neighborhood, I continued to think about Bettye. It was as though I was mourning.

The director of Prevention, Inc. tried to get us together. We met together with him. But I had hurt her so deeply; there was little that I could say. She made the remark that she would not even spit on me! It seemed that this was the *end* of our little courtship and relationship. Looking back, recently, I see what we should have done. I should have told Bettye about my reaction to Romans 14, and hopefully, we should have waited, prayerfully, until God worked in my parent's hearts to accept her. So I confess again. I behaved very wrongly, naively, and immaturely. I am sorry, particularly that I needlessly hurt Bettye so much. I repent, even now, although it is too late.

I had been working as an evangelist with the Assemblies of God and had an engagement to preach at a church in Eldora, Iowa. Somehow, it turned out that the pastor was leaving the church, and they called me as pastor. My parents were glad, believing I would forget about Bettye in this new position. I started in September, right after my fortieth birthday.

However, although I started with a week of Revival Services, since the church had not heard much of my preaching, nevertheless, I could not forget Bettye. I listened to Christian radio programs, and they all seemed to be telling me, spiritually, that she was still the one for me. The church had an adjoining chapel, where I liked to go to seek the Lord, and increasingly, He seemed to be showing me that she would yet be my wife.

Finally, I called a mutual friend and asked if she thought Bettye would be receptive to a call from me. She answered that she felt Bettye would welcome my call.

I determined, however, that I would never again desert or drop her, as I did before. And she did, indeed, welcome my call. It seemed that God was working at both ends! I told her I would stop by to see her on my way home for Thanksgiving.

We began corresponding and running up our phone bills! Our letters also soon turned into *love letters!* (But I never formally proposed to her.)

When I stopped to see her at Thanksgiving, she cooked breakfast for me. Then I asked her, "*What do you think our children will look like?*" (Later, I called that my proposal.) Bettye did not answer my question, but she did not say, "No. No!" So, we began planning our wedding.

We were married on December 23, 1969, at the Ezzard Charles Presbyterian Church, on the South Side of Chicago.

My mother had said that she would kill herself if I married Bettye! Later she said, "If you do marry her, don't tell us about it." I took her at her word and did as she said. But someone called her and asked where to send their wedding gift. This, of course, shocked and saddened my parents. But later, after my father's death, she began visiting us every week or two. Earlier, she had written me a note, saying, "It's your life. Do what you want with it."

When Mom was ninety-eight or ninety-nine years of age, she could no longer care for herself. Her bones were no longer making blood, and she grew tired of taking transfusions and stopped taking them. We took her in, and Bettye took care of her. Her doctor told her she would only live a few weeks, without transfusions. But Bettye took care of her for five months.

History repeated itself. My grandmother was cared for, by my mother, her daughter-in-law, in her last days. She dropped her disrespect for Mom and called her "my Angel." It was a similar experience, when Bettye took care of her. Mom called Bettye "her angel" and said, "I believe just like Bettye." I don't know exactly what she meant, but in her last days, she mentioned the "tall blonde in the back," behind us, as we talked to her. I'm sure she was talking about an angel, as that is their job to bring us to Heaven, the Presence of the Lord! We saw no tall blonde in the room.

Back to our wedding. Paul Evans, who later became our pastor, was assigned to me as mentor for our marriage. There had been a prophecy at the wedding that Bettye would be responsible if there were problems in our marriage. (Whether this was a legitimate prophecy or not is doubtful, as there was no regimen in the church, to try the prophecies, which were abundant in that church.) Bettye, understandably, was *very upset* that *she* should be responsible for our marriage, with no such word directed at me.

A few days after the wedding, Paul asked me if I wanted to get an annulment of the marriage. I was very surprised by that question and replied, "No, absolutely not! I didn't marry her to get an annulment!" She had criticized my driving, which I did not take to heart, as I *had* made a couple of mistakes.

After that, Bettye went out by herself, without saying anything to me, and stayed out several hours, until after nine p.m. I really had thought, perhaps she was going to leave me! But she didn't. Very sensitive to her leaving like this, without any word to me, *twice* I called the police, thinking I should file a missing person report! But of course, she returned later, as if it was nothing important and very surprised at me, for making it such an issue!

We had our lovers' spats, especially in the first year. I quickly learned that there was no way I could win an argument with her, as I was not an argumentative person. So when we had a disagreement, I would take a walk. That went on, at least during our first year.

Bettye said I was leaving the field of conflict or something like that. She said we needed to *communicate.* That sounded good to me, but I quickly learned that her definition of communication was different than mine, at least in practice. It meant, *she talked and I listened!*

After a few years of the above, I learned to "speak the truth in love" (Eph. 4:15). For example, if I forgot to bring something home from the store, I *deliberately* did so, in her mind. There was no two ways about it! Looking back, it was my fault because if I just had made a list and kept diligent track of it, the disagreements could have been eliminated. But I usually bought, just a few things and thought (wrongly) that I would not forget.

So in any disagreement, I would say just one sentence or two at the most to "defend myself." Then I would say, "I am sorry." And I truly was, for forgetting or doing anything to offend her.

But I also had to learn not to say, "*I'm sorry.*" Because every time I said it, she would counter with such words as "Sorry said is not always sorry meant." But I did learn that my short words sometimes got across to her, although it took some time. One thing about my darling Bettye was that she would always repent and admit her wrong, if she truly believed she *was* wrong.

I also soon learned that Bettye, sometimes, liked to talk our (or her) problems out, when we were in bed at night. There were times when I was very tired and thought, "If only she would be quiet, so I could sleep!" But, lo and behold! After talking it all out, with little or no comment from me, for (it seemed like) three hours, she was *satisfied*! The problem was solved! Her problem, I thought, because I didn't understand why she had a problem.

It sounds like I'm blaming Bettye for everything, as if I had no problems, but I *did* have *a problem,* which was, I was not a strong, authoritative husband and father. But I didn't recognize that problem, at least, at first. Bettye thought I should push myself, make myself known, as a preacher, that I should give people "a piece of my mind," if they were not acting right or if they offended us in any way. But it just was not my nature. I was not brought up that way. But I must confess that I was not a strong husband and father figure. And later, this led me to resign as a pastor because I could not adequately control my family.

At the same time, as I have already said, that if I was to preach, that was *all* that was on my mind. As we drove to church, Bettye would feel that there was something not right between us. I don't know what it was. And she could not understand that there was nothing on my mind, but the awesome privilege and responsibility to *proclaim the Word of God to needy souls for the glory of God.* There was room for nothing else in my heart and mind and soul, at that moment.

I'm not saying that other things were not important, that our marriage relationship was not of importance, second only to our relationship to our Great God and Savior, Our Lord Jesus Christ. But that and everything else must wait.

I must give an example of something that happened years later when our first daughter, Mary, was in high school. She was charged with excessive tardiness (between classes), and we went to see the principal about it. For some reason, Bettye took a neighbor with us. Her daughter was Mary's friend.

As we sat at the table with the principal, I was ashamed at the way the two women were railing at the principal. I had been brought up to respect authority. Suddenly, the principal slammed his fist on the table, scolding the women for trying to scold him. But I was accused of being weak and not defending my wife, which then became a constant charge against me. (However, because they had first yelled at the principal, I felt that there was little I could say in their defense.)

Nevertheless, some of our lovers' spats were almost worth it because it was so sweet to make up afterward. I remember leaving Bettye during our first year of marriage. I can't remember why, but I took my Bible and walked down Michigan Avenue until I came to a skid row hotel. I paid the night there and got on my knees to pray and read my Bible before I went to bed. I believe I was reading in Isaiah 44:22, "Return unto Me," but I could not sleep. I turned this way and that, but I heard "Return, go back! Return! Go back!"

I felt the Lord was saying to me, "Return to Bettye." I got up, dressed, and left the hotel. When I got home, Bettye had put furniture in front of the door to keep me out, but when she heard me at the door, she moved the furniture away and let me in! I think it was one of the sweetest times of our lives, as I took her in my arms! For we truly loved one another!

MIRACULOUS CHILDREN

All our children were *miraculous*, and here is why! The doctors had told Bettye that she could not have any more children because her glandular system was unbalanced. She had an overactive thyroid gland.

However, she had an evangelist friend, Brother Lee, who used to stay at her house, with Sister Cokes, Bettye's Godmother, on the West Side. He was in town to preach revivals. Bettye told

Evangelist Lee that the doctors said *she could not have children*. He answered with what we took as "the Word of the Lord." He said, *"You be faithful to God, and He will be faithful to you."*

We both believed that Word. It was about four months later when Bettye seemed to be getting sick again. So we went to a doctor, who told us her "sickness" was a three-month fetus. Looking back, we determined she must have conceived less than a month after receiving the Word of the Lord from Evangelist Lee!

But she had a hard pregnancy, so I took her to the *Illinois Research Hospital*, on the West Side. While she was there, the doctor asked her, "How could you be pregnant, after having a goiter? What 'wonder drug' was used? Why did you get pregnant?"

They told her they would do their best to keep her alive, but the medical treatment they proposed might kill the baby. We discussed this possibility and both agreed that we would sign her out, rather than put her baby at risk, although it was *against medical opinion*!

At that time, there was a *Home Maternity Program* on Maxwell Street on the near West Side. I took Bettye there, and when her birth pangs began, they sent nurses to be with her. (All her pregnancies were hard.) She "labored" all night, having had five nurses with her. Finally, the doctor was called.

I was called in to observe the birth of our first daughter. And I saw her before Bettye did! Coming out of her mother, looking like *me*. That was my first reaction. We felt that she was a beautiful, happy girl and named her *Mary Ruth*, the name God gave her, way before she was born, after the women in the Bible, Mary and Ruth. It was our intention that she was to be like those women.

Later, she was given another middle name, Qualla, by a Nigerian couple. It means the *peace after a storm*. And that is exactly how it was with Bettye, as the Bible says, she forgot the hard labor she had, for the *joy* that a little girl was born into the world (John 16:21, KJV)! In the next few years, she would be joined by our son, *David Jonathon* (names also given by God), and our youngest and last daughter, *Rebecca Therese*.

All our children were special *miracles*, as we had to leave Illinois Research Hospital, lest they killed our first child in trying to save Bettye! And since she was able to have the first, we were confident that God would give her more!

During her senior year of high school, Mary, now with a driver's license, took our car to visit Bettye, who was in the hospital. She was cut off by another driver on the expressway and, to avoid hitting the car, drove off the expressway, smashing into a tree! She was hospitalized with a hip bone broken in several places. She was told that she would not be able to walk to get her diploma. But she walked with a crutch for a while, and when graduation day came, she walked *without a crutch* to get her diploma!

BETTYE'S SPIRITUAL AND EDUCATIONAL BACKGROUND

Bettye entered Moody Bible Institute as a day student in 1963. Because of various sicknesses, she had to switch to the evening school. We attended her graduation party at the end of January 1970, only about one month after our wedding. She often talked about her classes, particularly in Evangelism, under Mr. Wemp.

Bettye's older sister, Nancy, who was chosen by their mother to take care of her (because her mother already had several children to care for) says that she was born sickly and was often sick. But she persevered and continued, just as she had done when she worked at the Curtiss Candy Company and other jobs. That is why it took her so long to finish, with a major in Christian Education and a minor in Missions.

She told me she went to Moody to make them rethink their position concerning black women, because MBI was educating them to be perhaps helpers to pastor husbands, Sunday school teachers, home missionaries, but *not* to be preachers or leaders in their churches.

Also, in those days, when they walked to classes, black students were to walk behind, not alongside white students. We must admit it was racism. It reminds me of the nonfraternization rules the American soldiers were said to be under, in parts of Germany, taken over by the Allies in the Second World War. Our government wanted no mishaps with the German girls!

So Bettye was sick at Moody, had an appendectomy and kidney problems. She says the Lord gave her "new kidneys" there. And it was no doubt true because she had little trouble with them for the next forty years.

Ms. Angela Dantuma, Dean of Women at Moody "took Bettye under her wing" and was very kind to her. Bettye was one of the few, if not the only, commuting student. Ms. Dantuma had Bettye report to her every morning, before classes, for prayer. She also told the women students to open their rooms to her, if she needed to rest between some of her classes.

CHILD EVANGELISM

During the summers of 1963–1965, Bettye was active in child evangelism, telling the story of Jesus to children in parks and starting clubs with them, using flannelgraph stories. She loved this work very much, winning many children to the Lord!

MICKEY

The story of Bettye's first daughter.

Since it is a matter of record, Bettye wrote about it in her book, *Through Much Tribulation, We Shall Overcome*, I will let you know that she was raped by a high school classmate, when she somehow got separated from her family at a county fair and was afraid she would not be able to find them. She reluctantly accepted a ride from two boys, who promised to bring her right to her family, but instead, they stopped, and one of them raped her. It was a very humbling experience for her, and it was many years and much suffering before she could forgive the man.

Of course, she told no one about the experience. That was not what you would do in the South, in Shaw, Mississippi, her home in those days! But later, she went to a doctor for a stomachache and was told that she was pregnant!

Her mother had said that if anything like that happened to any of her girls, she would put them out! She did not. But she did want to take her to the boy and make him marry her, to save face!

But she did not! Bettye said she would rather marry her cat or dog! She did not even want to walk on the same side of the street, if she saw him coming! But her father soon came to her rescue and insisted she did not have to marry the boy. (She was only sixteen!) But her life was changed forever!

One of her brothers wanted to give her a pill that supposedly would abort the baby. I don't know if it would have worked, but on the advice of an older sister, she refused the pill as it would have been murder if it had worked. There would have been no *Annie Louise Baker*, born on May 30, 1953, or any of her five children and three grandchildren! And of course, I would, no doubt, have never met and married her mother, as I would not have been her teacher! *All praise to our great God and heavenly Father!*

When she was a little girl, someone jokingly called her "Mickey," thinking she looked like Mickey Mouse, the Walt Disney cartoon character! And the nickname stuck to this very day! I "inherited" her as my daughter when I married her mother. She has been a wonderful daughter, never gave us any trouble and was not worldly.

Bettye, however, had to "kidnap" her from her mother, once she (Bettye) got saved and felt it was her responsibility to take care of her own daughter. Her mother wanted to adopt her, perhaps because of an "empty nest syndrome." But Bettye took her and led her to the Lord, at twelve years of age. (You can read the details in Bettye's book.)

CHAPTER 9

HEALING AND OTHER MIRACLES

Perhaps because of the stress I had put her through, in abruptly leaving Prevention Inc., Bettye developed a goiter (enlarged thyroid gland) on her neck. It was not huge, but you could see it protruding.

After our wedding, she began to itch all over her body. At home, she would take off most of her clothes, because of the itching. Also, she could not walk more than a half a block, without becoming breathless.

The devil, through an evil spirit of suicide, tempted her to do away with herself! She had been troubled before by just such a spirit. She sat on the overpass, above the expressway, and the devil told her to jump down and let the cars run over her and put her out of her misery. But thank God, she did not listen to Satan!

Now she was tempted again. We had moved to a high-rise at 20th and South Michigan Avenue, which had windows from the floor to the ceiling, in the living room. Again, the enemy tempted her to throw herself out against the windows to fall to the ground (as we lived on the 28th floor), and if she could just crash through the permanent windows and fall to the ground, she would surely die! I praise our great God again! She resisted Satan again, and said no!

For she felt that she would be guilty of murder, by taking her own life and, being dead, could not even repent. (Let me say here that God is the judge of all such suicides, and I believe, very probably, many of them are not in "their right mind," and therefore, are forgiven by the grace of God, if they were among those of us who trust Jesus Christ and His atonement for us on the cross, for our Eternal Salvation.)

However, we went to a doctor for treatment and he apparently proposed *chemotherapy* for Bettye, which may have made her sterile, concerning childbirth. But she did not want to take it, for my sake, because I wanted children. It is true that I mentioned children, as the natural result of marriage, in my "marriage proposal," but we had never discussed it since then.

At any rate, Bettye decided not to return to that doctor. I even stayed home from work one day to make sure she would go to some doctor. But it happened to be a Wednesday, and at that time, I did not realize that most doctors were not in their offices on Wednesdays.

It was then September, and the doctor called her, asking her *why* she didn't keep her appointment. Bettye replied that she was just going to trust God. "What are you going to do?" he chided. "Become a Christian Scientist, or something?"

"No," she answered, "I am just going to trust God."

That was when the agitated doctor yelled, "Don't you know that unless you get in here and get therapy, you won't see Christmas!"

This statement by the doctor upset my darling, somewhat. But she was firm in her decision to trust God. She told me the Lord had told her, "If you trust in the doctors, you *will* die, but if you trust Me, you will live."

I must add here, that this word from the Lord was not a universal principle, but at this time, God wanted her to trust in Him alone. I say this because, for years, later, Bettye took plenty of medicine, from prescriptions, for the Lord told her later, "Let the doctors heal what they can heal, but I specialize in the impossible."

So we decided, together, to go on a three-day fast, eating nothing. And I drank nothing. I didn't know, until some years later, that Christian authorities recommend that you should drink water freely on a fast and should not stop taking any medicine that you have been taking.

Although I have known people who tell of taking forty-day fasts, it was hard enough for me to go three days while I was still working at the Urban Progress Center at 47th and King Drive, as a Neighborhood Youth Counselor for the Illinois State Job Service.

The 58th chapter of Isaiah gives good advice about fasting. The *motive* of our fast is all important. It should be for the *blessing of people* and the *glory of God*, not to prove how great we are in refusing our necessary food, but a time to devote ourselves to God and not our own devices or efforts!

At the end of our three-day fast, I made my way up to the 28th floor of our twenty-nine-floor high-rise, which I called HALF-WAY TO HEAVEN and announced to Bettye, my beloved, that I *knew* that God was going to heal her. She responded that she also *knew* that God would heal her.

A few weeks later, some of the sainted women from our church and from a West Side prayer group decided to pray all night for Bettye. They put her in a bed and began praying. I was there and prayed for her, but then went home, as I had to go to work the next day. But the women continued to pray all night.

HOW I KNEW BETTYE WAS HEALED

As I saw her every day, it was hard to tell for sure that she was healed. But it seemed to me that the enlarged gland was getting slightly smaller. Then something unusual happened. Somehow, we got a table. I forget if it was from a garage sale or was given to us. Bettye wanted to paint it for Thanksgiving. She loved to do things like that. But she stayed up until late at night, the night before Thanksgiving, painting the table we would use for Thanksgiving dinner. She painted it a Chinese red color! (I can still see it now, in my mind.) She said nothing about being healed, but she could never have done so a couple of months before!

In those days, I had an extra job on Saturdays, working at Marshall Fields, downtown, as mentioned earlier. But one Saturday, *Bettye met me for lunch*! She had walked all the way downtown! About twenty or more blocks! Maybe two and a half miles! *How we rejoiced and praised God!* There was no doubt about her healing now!

OTHER HEALINGS

One Sunday, when our son, David, was perhaps four years old, he was sick in bed. He was listless, not playing with his toys. But we went to church. I can't remember for sure, but perhaps, it was our daughter, Annie, who stayed with him.

I was given the opportunity, occasionally, to speak in the church we attended at that time, so I preached that Sunday on "soul winning." When we got home, instead of eating or taking care of her son, Bettye immediately went down the street and began witnessing. She very soon came to a home in need. She prayed for a sick lady who was then healed! For the next several years, we ministered to that household!

When she got home, David, who had been sick in bed, was now up playing with his toys! He was healed! Although she said nothing about why she had left her sick son to go witnessing, I believe Bettye felt that if she took care of God's business, God would take care of *her* "business." Of course, we praised the Lord, not only for healing our son, but also the neighbor lady! I do not now remember her malady.

When our youngest daughter, Rebecca, was just in grade school, she went to a summer camp and somehow had a broken finger. She did not tell us about it because she didn't want to have to come home before the camp was over.

Later, we took her to a luncheon held by Evangelist Morris Cerullo, in hopes that she would be healed. And sure enough, during the testimonies and prayers, sitting right at our table, the finger which was out of place, suddenly snapped right back in place! Praise our great and good God!

DAVID HEALED OF BRAIN DAMAGE

We moved to Mobile, Alabama, by prophecy, in about 1991. This is how it happened. A friend of Bettye's asked her if she knew anyone named Dick. She said, "Yes, my husband."

The lady replied, "Then, you are going to move somewhere, where it is very warm, and *palm* trees grow."

We felt surely that it was a word from the Lord, but we didn't know where to go. So we, and particularly Bettye, began praying. Sometime later, she asked me if I knew of any place called Mobile, but she pronounced it like "mobul."

I said, "You must mean Mobile [Alabama]."

Just about that time, we heard from a lady in our church, who had moved to Mobile and found a good church there. So we decided to take a trip to investigate and see if this could be the place where we were to move. We arrived in Mobile after dark, so we found a motel for the night.

When we woke up in the morning, we looked out of the windows, and *lo and behold*, what did we see? *Palm trees!* So with our friend in a good church, which we visited, and the palm trees, we felt this must be the place! We made plans to move.

We were going to rent our condo in University Park (Illinois) to a lady with a son about David's age, and David was going to stay for his senior year in high school. But, at the last day, David decided to go with us – Bettye and I and Rebecca. Mary was already married.

We were a little worried about David. We were just a few miles from where the Klu Klux Klan originated and didn't know how David would do. He had earlier joined a gang in University

Park, unbeknownst to us. Somehow, he had given away the gang sign at a party. The penalty was a beating by the gang. Several of them came to our door with bats and clubs! But Bettye was not afraid of them! She said, "I know every one of you, and if anything happens to David, I'll give your names to the police, and you better never come back here with those bats!" And they all walked away, and never came back!

A neighbor man heard it all and said, "Mrs. Lythberg, don't you know who those boys were?"

Bettye replied, "I don't care who they are. I'm not afraid of them!"

Nevertheless, David hid from them all that summer, as they only had a certain amount of time to get him, according to the gang rules! We put him in another school the next fall, until the police told us that those boys had been "sent down the river." But as it turned out, he became very popular in the new school in Mobile, both with boys and girls. However, some of them seemed to be party boys and "gothic" girls, who wore black clothes.

To shorten the story, David got with the "party boys" and was forbidden by his mother from leaving his room one Saturday. But he climbed out of a window and met his friends. They only went a couple of blocks, when the driver of their car reached down for a bottle of pop, while crossing a busy street. An open truck, full of youngsters headed for their car. The driver later said he was afraid to put on the brakes because the children would fall out of the truck.

The boys' car ended up rammed against a telephone post. It was a hatch back. David was knocked unconscious. Another boy was knocked out of the car. A helicopter came from the University of South Alabama and took David to their hospital, since he was unconscious.

Unfortunately, the other boy was taken to another hospital, where he died that night! One of the mothers called Bettye, who did not even know David was gone, to tell her that he was taken to a hospital, but she did not know which one! She took Bettye to the city's hospitals, one by one. I did not go as they said only one person would be allowed to see the patients.

They took her to one hospital, but Bettye said, "That is not my son, as his head was swollen to twice its size." But then she remembered how David used to dye his hair, and she saw a little red in his hair, so she went back—and oh my God! *It was David!*

He was in a coma, which I believe, lasted about two weeks. We stayed all night with him praying and trying to sleep on a couple of chairs. I stayed only a night or two. I couldn't take trying to sleep on a couple of chairs.

But Bettye, with a mother's heart, stayed for almost a week, praying for her son. Finally, I persuaded her to come home, take a rest and a shower. She had called a friend, who was called a prophet, to pray for him. He said, "Just a minute" and went away to pray. He came back to the phone and announced that our son was going to die! But we would not accept that! We continued to pray and believe.

Many came in from the church we now attended, Life Church, under Pastor Dick Braswell, to pray for him. But with all the suffering (a trachea cut had been made in his neck, to help his breathing), there is a humorous story about how he "woke up" or began to wake up. The doctor put the phone up to his ear, saying, "David, you have a call!" And he grabbed the phone, saying, "Hello!"

Soon after that, I began walking him around the hospital, none of which he could remember later. The doctor, however, told us that severe damage had been done by bleeding in his brain. He told us that he would never be able to return to high school because he would not remember what classes to go to, when the bell rang, neither would he be able to hold a job!

But we, especially Bettye, his mother, would not accept that! When he could have visitors, his new friends came, saying, "Hurry up, and get well, so we can party!" Then the weird girls came, dressed in black! We were afraid that they might be putting curses on him, so we barred all visitors.

He then was moved to a rehab center, like a nursing home. There he had speech therapy and other tests, which we were told, indicated he had the intelligence of an eleven-year-old, but he would never go above that!

We refused to believe their tests! But continued to pray. For a while, a special teacher came from the high school to tutor him. Soon, however, he returned to the high school, where he not only was graduated but won a writing contest, held by a local university. David then began taking classes at the University of South Alabama.

Isn't God good? He heard our prayers! When we moved back to the Chicago area, he continued taking college classes, and he *has held jobs* and has been working ever since! His healing was not perfect, in that, for several years, he would have occasional migraine headaches, but as I write, he seldom has those headaches. PRAISE GOD!

REVELATIONS AND DREAMS GIVEN TO BETTYE

Bettye was sensitive to evil spirits, and even saw them at times! But she had a fear of them! I somehow did not often have this sensitivity, but I was not afraid of them, knowing they must be obedient to Christ Jesus and His Word.

A sister of the lady who was healed, when Bettye visited them (mentioned previously) came to our house on Christmas Eve, telling us she was to be married the next day, Christmas Day.

But instead of rejoicing with her, as she probably expected, the Spirit of Prophecy came upon Bettye and she gave her words that were, no doubt, hard to say. (I would not say that Bettye was a prophetess, but when that spirit comes upon you, you must not be "afraid of their faces" [Jer. 1:8].)

Bettye told her, "If you marry that man"—whom we had never seen, nor knew anything about—"you will have sorrow upon sorrow."

And although we prayed, she went ahead and married the man, and that was *exactly what happened!* She had sorrow upon sorrow, for several years, without going into any details, until finally, their marriage improved.

In another case, Bettye had a dream about another lady friend of ours who was about to be married. The dream was about a picnic, where Bettye said to the lady, "This is phony baloney!" I told her she had better tell the lady about the dream, as it seemed to be from the Lord.

She did, and the outcome of the marriage was that the husband turned out to be a homosexual, and it is doubtful if they ever had normal sexual relations. And the marriage did not last long.

CHAPTER 10

"ANGELS" AND "DEMONS"

I did have some bad experiences—robbed of my car (twice), robbed of my wallet in the vestibule of our apartment, threatened by a young man as I crossed the street in front of our house, a flat tire on a dark night in a black neighborhood, etc. But I believe most of them were orchestrated by God to show how He loves us and how He can protect us in dangerous situations.

I was very naive in the early days of our marriage. I would take walks at eleven o'clock at night, in the midst, you might say, of "gangland," on the South Side of Chicago. I didn't realize what chances I was taking. If you have had your car stolen, you might know how I felt.

The first time was while working for Illinois Job Service. A young man named Charles, who had been in my class in eighth grade, came to see me in my office at the Urban Progress Center at 47th and King Drive. I was wearing a suit coat and unwisely left my car keys in the coat, which I had taken off and hung on the back of my chair. I went away from my desk and Charles, momentarily, for some reason.

By the end of the day, I realized my keys were gone! Then I went to my car and found that it was *gone,* too! I thought back and realized that the only time I left my coat unattended was when Charles was there! It was many years ago, as I write, but I believe I called him and told him of my missing car *and missing keys,* from the time he was in my office, but he denied taking the keys and the car.

Several days later, he called me, saying he saw my car parked at a certain place. I was about to go there and get it (as I had another pair of keys), but Charles called back, telling me he was mistaken. It was not my car. By that time, I was pretty sure Charles had stolen my car!

Now, I had taught this young man how to drive! He weighed about two hundred pounds at the time and could outrun me, although I was in my early forties and could run fairly fast! We used to box for fun, but Charles hit me once in the chest. And I thought he had broken my rib! I went to the hospital later and found it was just a bruise.

Despite all this, I forgave him, and Charles became one of my "angels." One of the men in our church used to call him my son. He called me again, saying he really saw my car, and I did recover it. But Charles never admitted that he took it, until just before he died from diabetes and further complications, about two years ago. I used to call Charles a fellow traveler, as I knew he wasn't saved, but he still loved to come to church and be among the believers!

Then, for many years, I lost track of Charles, and when I saw him again, I knew there had been a change in his life. He truly loved to come to church and praise the Lord, but now, he was in a wheelchair and needed assistance. He told me what had happened to him. He had been on drugs and was homeless. He would travel back and forth on the "El" trains at night. But one night, a lady, who had a radio program on WYCA, out of Hammond, Indiana, found him and led him to the Lord! *Praise God!* He got cleaned up and God blessed him to start a moving company, and he prospered for several years.

But even before he knew the Lord, he was my "angel," as I would go in the projects to witness to the people, he would be with me. When I would take the elevators, I know, by the way some tough guys looked at me, I would be a "goner," if it wasn't for

Charles being with me! Also, several times he went with me as I would pass out tracts and preach at the "El" station at 95th Street.

The one case that was most like a real angel, except that it was a *dog*, a police dog, that walked along with me for about two blocks, when I left our church, meeting in a home, late at night. The dog did not bark, but walked beside me on the grass, while I walked on the sidewalk. When I got to a big street, where I could get a bus, the dog stopped, turned around, and walked away, as if it had done its duty, protecting a white man in a black neighborhood until I could get a bus.

Speaking of buses, I was in trouble, soon after our marriage. Bettye had left her Bible at a prayer meeting at a church near the United Center, famous for its sports events. I had retrieved her Bible and was waiting for a bus, across the street from the Center, in front of a tavern. There were two black fellows in a corner, talking, while I stood by the curb, waiting for a bus. Finally, one of them came over to me, saying, "My friend wanted to jump on you, but I told him you were a friend of mine."

He stood there with me, as if he was waiting for the bus, too. But when it came, he did not get on. He waved and said, "Take care of yourself."

Another similar case was also in front of a tavern. I suddenly had a flat tire on a very dark night, in a black neighborhood. There were four or five fellows talking there and expressing an interest in my plight. They offered to change tires for me, as I had a spare in the trunk. I had, I think, six dollars in my wallet.

When they finished, I thanked them and told them, probably unwisely, that I had six dollars, and asked if five was enough for them. The one who seemed to be the leader, said, "I think you better give us all of it."

I said, "Yeah, I think you are right." And I thanked them and God for their kindness. Of course, I knew that if God were not in our midst, the outcome could have been very different.

And there was a case or two, where the outcome *was* different, unfortunately. I had become assistant pastor to Brother Jesse Norwood in a church in Gary, Indiana. He, I, and two or three other leaders were holding Bible studies in homes of new members. We were going in pairs but had an uneven number. Big? Brave? Dumb! Me! I volunteered to go alone, stupidly.

I was looking for an address in an area that I did not realize was a very dangerous part of town. Hardheaded, I learned the hard way! I got out of my car to ask someone on the street for help in finding an address. Mistake number one!

There were two men walking toward me. One was tall. One was short. The tall man pulled out a gun and demanded my keys. "You aren't going to take my car, are you, fellows?"

My question was ignored. By this time, the tall guy had handed the gun to the short one, while he was taking my car. It was a cold winter day, about zero degrees! I tried to be brave! I tried to call on the Lord, but I was scared! I might as well admit it! In fact, to be honest, I peed in my pants! (Big, brave me!)

The little guy told me to look the other way, as the big guy was starting my car. I kept turning my head. I couldn't believe it! Someone was stealing my car! He kept hitting me on the head with the gun! I felt nothing! Finally, the little guy was pointing the gun at me with a shaking hand! Saying accidents do happen! (He was pleading with me to be quiet or he was going to shoot me!)

Then they were gone, and my car was gone! And I was standing on a cold street in Gary, Indiana. Somehow, I got to a police station to report the robbery. There was no "angel" this time! The police did call me a few days later, telling me they had found and recovered my car! Thank God! There were some things missing. But the car was in fairly good shape.

I was asked to come in and look at a lineup to see if I could identify anyone. I did and pointed out what looked like the "little guy." *Thank You, Jesus!* I got my car back! I don't know what happened to either of the two guys. I never heard any more and never got back the things missing from the car. But I was beginning to learn some lessons.

I think it was about 1974. We had another bad winter with a lot of snow. We lived on the southeast side. Somehow "our" car, I *should* say, got stuck in the alley, and then there was more snow.

So for two or three weeks, I had to take public transportation to work at the Urban Progress Center at 47th and King Drive. And it was so crowded with people trying to get on the bus, due to the weather that I had to walk another block or two, to get on the bus before it filled up.

I guess it was a Saturday, when I was off, I decided I better do something to try and get our snowbound auto free. There were many others in the same predicament at that time, as I said, due to the weather. So when I got to my car, I saw a bunch of neighborhood Winos with shovels, helping people get their cars free.

There were about a half dozen of them. And they were very nice and glad to get the five or ten dollars I gave them, as they soon got the car free. It was not a time to do much witnessing to them. And I do not remember ever seeing them again.

Speaking of bad experiences, I had another, in that same neighborhood. It was probably the summer following that snowy winter. I had just gotten paid and walked to the neighborhood Jewel store to get some groceries. I saw some tough looking guys outside the store, looking at me. I thought, *Oh, oh*, but began walking rapidly toward home. I didn't see anyone following me, so I thought I was free. As I opened the door to the vestibule, out of nowhere, a young guy grabbed me from behind and was trying to yank the wallet out of my pocket.

I knew that Matthew 5:39 says that we should not resist evil, but it was a gut reaction. I turned and put my foot in the guy's midsection. I must have yelled because our friend, Emelda, on the first floor (of the three-flat) came out, yelling at the man. But he was gone, and so was my wallet!

Providentially, I had emptied my wallet before leaving and took just enough money for the groceries. Thank God. However, I finally was learning something. After that, I became very careful about where I was and who was behind me, even going into a public bathroom. But my wallet and all my IDs were gone. I don't remember reporting it to the police. Perhaps I should have.

ED TAYLOR

One of my angels was Edwin Taylor, already mentioned as assistant pastor of the church we attended, organist, and youth worker in the church and in the street. It was said that Ed knew and witnessed to hundreds of "gang boys."

Naively, I was still witnessing in the black neighborhood. I was passing out notices, door-to-door, of a revival meeting we were having, when I was stopped by a young tough-looking guy. He said to this white-skinned guy, "What are you doing in this neighborhood?"

I told him about the revival meetings. He did not seem interested or impressed. So, knowing I was in trouble, I blurted out, "*I know Ed Taylor!*"

"You know Ed Taylor?" he asked incredulously!

"Yes," I said, "He is a friend of mine."

Ed's reputation was such that just the *mention of his name* was like an *angel* that saved me! He let me go to continue advertising the Revival.

JOE AND THE GANG CLUB

As I was teaching seventh and eighth grades in the Evangelical Christian School, I realized that some of the boys had problems and needed discipline. We were given paddles and instructed to give demerits, calling for their hands to be paddled if pupils did not obey us. I hated to do so. There was no law against corporal punishment, apparently, in those days.

I decide to start a *Boys Club* on one night of the week, to influence the boys and get on better rapport with them.

As already mentioned, someone had given me a wrestling mat, which I used for a similar club as pastor of the Bethany Baptist Church on Chicago's Near South Side. We had many neighborhood boys coming to the club, until someone spray-painted on the walls! This caused our deacons and deaconesses board to call for an end to the club. But I still had the mat, so we used it for the club.

Roger McGowan, a member of the Evangelical Christian Church and a good friend of mine, apparently told two of his younger brothers about the club. The only problem about that was they did not go to our school, but they were Cobrastones (members of the Youth Adjunct of the notorious gang of the time, the Blackstone Rangers)! They came to the first meeting and brought some of their friends. I only remember two other boys from the school ever coming. With the gang boys coming, the school boys were afraid to come! So...I had a "Gang Club." But I was not about to stop the Cobrastones from coming, as this was, no doubt, an opening from the Lord, to reach them.

Joe McGowan was not tall, but wiry, about sixteen years old. His younger brother was David Earl. In addition to wrestling on the mat, they would spontaneously put on skits of the police coming, stopping them, searching them, etc. The skits were very good. But when it came time to open the Bible, Joe would make sure "his boys" got quiet and listened to the Word.

Sometimes, I visited the gang boys' clubhouse or saw them on the streets, when the police *did* stop to question them. Once, one of their friends from another gang, which was rare, apparently had too much wine and wanted to fight me, but Joe wouldn't let him! I also took them to Stateville Prison at Joliet, Illinois, to see one of their friends. Another time, Roger and I were going to watch a "rumble" (fight) with a rival gang. I was a bit scared as we waited by a nearby viaduct. But thank God, they called the rumble off.

Bettye and I loved the boys, especially Joe, so when I heard that Nicky Cruz was advertising rallies on the North Side, I invited the boys to come. (Nicky had been a member of the wild Mau Mau Gang in New York, coming from Puerto Rico, who got saved under David Wilkerson, the founder of Teen Challenge, an organization which worked with drug addicts.) The story was told in the movie, *The Cross and the Switchblade*, starring Pat Boone, and later in Nicky's book, *Run, Baby, Run.* As Nicky became an evangelist in California.

When Nicky gave the invitation to accept Christ as Savior, after telling his story, the boys did not move. Finally, I asked Joe, "Why don't you just go up there and talk to them?" And he did! Just needed a little "push."

On the way to the rally, the boys were singing worldly songs, but on the ride home, they were singing Christian songs! I assumed that Joe, at least, had accepted Christ as His Savior! I knew that Joe was going to have to face some new decisions he had never faced before, now as a Christian! I told him that we needed to pray. But he replied, "Don't worry about me. I'll be all right." However, it is not so easy to leave the gang, once you are in it. Joe did not leave. He said they had no one else to lead them, but him.

I heard that the gang had pulled a robbery the very next week. I think school was out for the summer, as I don't remember continuing with the club.

Sometime later, it seems that the "friend" from a rival gang betrayed Joe to them. A gun was pointed at him, and he was told to walk away, which he refused to do, knowing they would shoot him in the back. Joe was shot dead!

I recently saw my friend, Roger, Joe's elder brother. He told me Joe would get down on his knees and pray every night! Even, as I write, I can hardly hold back the tears! If only I could have done more to help Joe! Perhaps he was afraid of the older Blackstone Rangers, if he would have left the gang!

In those days, many people prayed, and the gangs subsided for a while, but now, years later, they are worse than ever, with many new gangs, shooting little children—*with guns they should not have! Let us pray again* for an end of racism and violence and gangs!

CHAPTER 11

AFRICA—A MIXED BAG

Bettye and I both felt we had a call to India, as foreign missionaries. She, I believe, because of the work of George Verwer, a student at the Moody Bible Institute, while she was also there. Bettye became a corresponding secretary for Verwer's "Send the Light" movement, which worked in India (and other foreign ports).

We had already gone, the previous year, to Kenya, in East Africa, for about a month, to participate in a nationwide youth conference. Kenya had proved to be a very beautiful country with rolling green fields of tea plantations. We stayed near Nairobi, also a beautiful capital city. We were invited by a seventy-year-old missionary, about to retire, looking for someone to take his place.

I would say that the country was not as advanced as those on the West Coast, at least as far as sewage and other conveniences. But the people were very nice. The two national Christian leaders we worked with were Patrick Ndirangu and Djiguna, who was teaching me the Trade Language, Swahili.

Patrick, though, seemingly a young mild-mannered man, was the leader over some thirty-eight or forty churches. And his wife was a principal of a Catholic Elementary School. In Africa, they do not seem to hold a big division between Catholic and protestant or Evangelical churches. In fact, the elected president of our first Bible School class in Ghana was a Roman Catholic.

There was political turmoil, even then, in Kenya. Besides that, I remember watching from an upper story window, to witness a huge crowd of people pursuing and capturing a thief. I was told that if the police did not intercede and take the man out of their hands, he was in danger of having his hand cut off, so he could no longer steal! (This, I understand, is a Muslim form of justice.)

We enjoyed the youth conference, especially how the young Christians prayed with their faces against the wall, fervently! But the African women would not believe that Bettye was an American! They did not know that America had black people. Since Bettye looked like them, they thought she was only pretending to be an American!

Our host, however, did not seem to favor women preachers. Finally, though, he relented, and allowed Bettye to speak in the street meetings, in which we participated. I spoke once or twice in the evening meetings. However, I was always glad to see Bettye go forth and preach. Later, she would be a very popular anointed preacher in Women's Aglow and other meetings.

While in Kenya, we became acquainted with the Masai Tribe, a peculiar tall people, who believed all the cattle in the world belonged to them. Therefore, if they "rescued" them, they were not cattle thieves! Also, they lived, primarily, on the blood and milk of the cattle!

Later, I got in touch with a Kenyan in Life Church, which we joined in Mobile, Alabama. He was to put me in touch with the Masai Christians, who were very nice (and jumped *high* in their praises, when they worshipped). However, unfortunately, some Masai (not Christians, of course) attacked the Kikouye Tribe, and I could not get in contact with them.

Our host in Kenya taught a class every Saturday to the Kenyan pastors. I was dissatisfied with the class, however, as it seemed like a Sunday school class. So I felt that the pastors needed something more like a Bible School, and that was my desire with the Masai pastors, but it never happened.

It was about a year later, when Bettye was grieving over her mother's death, when she asked a missionary friend, named

Clara, why she had not left for Ghana, West Africa (where we had heard she was going). She stunned her by saying, "I have been waiting for you, to go with me. I want a preaching lady to accompany me."

I said, "It is OK with me, if you want to go."

Bettye said, "Thanks for volunteering me!" But after prayer, she felt it was the Lord's will, despite her mother's recent death. It was good for her, although she got deathly sick on the trip home and almost had to stay in London before God rather miraculously healed her.

But while in Africa, Bettye asked me to pray about coming to Ghana, since the opening to minister to the Masai pastors seemed to have blown away. I never did hear from the man in charge of the Masai work. So I prayed, and indeed, I seemed to hear the Macedonian call. *"And a vision appeared to Paul in the night; there stood a man of Macedonia, and prayed him, saying, 'Come over into Macedonia, and help us. And after he had seen the vision, immediately we endeavored to go into Macedonia, assuredly gathering that the Lord had called us for to preach the Gospel unto them."* (Acts 16:9,10, KJV)

I believe it was later the same year that I went alone to Ghana, to "lay the ground work," to secure a place to live, and to get acquainted with the Christian work already established there. I went to Takoradi (the second city to Accra, the capital, which had a population of more than one million people).

Since I could not contact the Masai in Kenya, Bettye told Pastor Joshua Holder, our contact in Ghana about it. And he said I could start a Bible School in Ghana. Holder was a pastor in Liberia, and had to leave amid gunfire (because of the civil war there), which wounded a young girl who was helping his family. The whole family, including small children, walked all the way across the *Ivory Coast*, since it was a French-speaking country, and they did not speak French, but wanted to reach Ghana, where the national language was English.

The first year in Ghana was very difficult because I had no material for the Bible School and had to write the courses myself.

I taught classes, such as Survey of the Old and New Testaments, including all the books of the Bible, Evangelism, and courses based on two books by Lee Strobel, *The Case for Christ* and *The Case for Faith*. Some courses I wrote, but did not teach, e.g., "leadership."

Since it would be too boring, if I taught *all* the courses, Joshua taught one class, and his friend, Leo taught Music, which is very necessary in the African church and evangelism. Bettye did not come to teach, but I pressed her into service. And she became an excellent teacher, particularly on the subject, "The Life of Christ," and she also taught "Spiritual Warfare."

We had classes only on Saturdays, as the students worked on the other days, and some walked a long way to come to class. We had just one young lady student (from Liberia). (I called her a rose among the thorns!) Her husband, who was also a student, had been one of the best tennis players in Liberia, and he gave Joshua and me some good tennis lessons. But I never got a chance to play tennis after that!

Rebecca, our youngest child, went with us that year as she was being "home schooled." She was very valuable and useful, in talking with the young people. She seldom asked us any questions about her work. Did it mostly on her own, from her books and material. Later that year, when we returned to "the States," we took her to Texas, where she was graduated from high school, with honors.

I really felt I was a missionary when we went to a remote village called Botadwina (pronounced Boat-uh-Joo-nuh). It reminded me of the pioneers in our country meeting with the Indian chiefs and smoking a peace pipe together. The African protocol, when visiting someone after a long trip is, after a few minutes of greetings, you are asked, "What is your mission?" Bettye was with me and Joshua Holder, the pastor of our host church. In addition to the chief or chiefs of the tribe, there is a spokesman, who can speak well and, in this case, who can speak English.

When the Spokesman asked us, "What is your mission?" I don't remember if Pastor Holder or I answered, but we asked them if they wanted us to help them to start a Christian church in their village. Their answer was *affirmative*, so we rejoiced and set about to do just that, *start a church!*

The part that Bettye and I were to take was to start a Bible School. So we began coming on a week night, every week. Traveling on the remote roads was dangerous, especially after a rain. In fact, one night our car hit a goat, in leaving the city. I felt very bad about it, but we had no time to stop. Several Ghanians told me, later, not to worry about it. The shepherds are supposed to take care of their animals and keep them from running out into the street.

Since few people in the village spoke English, we had only a few young people in the Bible School. But they were diligent and wanted to learn, and we wanted to teach them!

Like all of us, despite taking the required preventive medicine, Rebecca got malaria, and to her alarm, we had to leave her for several hours in a clinic, while we went to some meeting. We all got malaria, and I was told *all* Ghanians (and probably all Africans) get malaria. You ask, "What is it like to have malaria?"

You do not want to get it to find out! It is like a very bad cold or case of influenza! You are full of fever and ache all over. You feel weak and light-headed, like you can hardly make it! At least, that is how it was with me! I think I changed my pajamas six times one night! Because I was sweating so much and was almost delirious! But thanks be to God, our great Savior! I only remember having it twice!

I must add that that first time I was sick, a Christian doctor volunteered to come to me and set up intravenous treatment from my bed, and I soon recovered! Thank God!

Round trip airline fares were more economical, so we planned several months in Ghana and, then, came home to see about our family, as later, we had grandchildren. This first time, however, Bettye and Rebecca left a month ahead, as I remained to hold a graduation ceremony for the Bible School.

I also appointed some teachers, in case we were not able to return. And that is what happened. Because of back problems,

Bettye was unable to return to Africa. She took the maximum of three pain relieving injections and then had successful spinal surgery, which revealed she had a fracture from a bus accident years earlier. Later, she also had knee surgeries, receiving artificial knees in both legs.

Finally, in December 1999, Bettye's niece, Queen Esther, who had married Paul Evans, who was then our pastor, asked her when she was going back to Africa. Bettye said, "When God supplies the money."

Queen replied, "You've got it!"

And that began several years that we were well funded by the New Covenant Bible Church, which later became the Anointed Heirs Outreach Ministries International (AHOMI) under Apostle Edward J. Anderson and Pastor L' Tonia Anderson, the daughter of Paul and Queen Esther.

Bettye went alone, back to Ghana, in 2000, and had a very successful ministry. She preached for Pastor Bristler at the Assembly of God in Daboase and was honored on her 64th birthday on May 25, 2000. Later she went to the Bimbilla Teachers College, in the northern region, where they loved her ministry, at their graduation, and she loved them! She was going to visit each of the grads, in their hometown, but her health and other circumstances, unfortunately, did not permit this.

We prayed the Jabez prayer. *"Now Jabez was more honorable than his brothers, and his mother called his name Jabez, saying, 'Because I bore him in pain.' And jabez called on the God of Israel, saying, 'Oh, that You would bless me, indeed, and enlarge my territory, that your hand would be with me. And that You would keep me from evil, that I may not cause pain!' So God granted him what he requested"* (1 Chron. 4:9, 10, NKJV).

And it seemed that God was blessing. We supported several pastors, had four Bible Schools going at one time, as well as a day school, and we thought, two orphanages, only to find out, one of them was not an orphanage but a day school because the pupils did not stay overnight, so they were not considered orphans, since, apparently relatives were supporting them.

That is why I called our time in Africa a mixed bag. We began to have problems with some of our pastors. We heard Evangelist Morris Cerullo say that many were ready to go out to their countrymen and preach the Gospel! That all they needed was someone to support them financially. But unfortunately, we supported some too well. We gave them one hundred dollars per month, and one was giving a much lesser amount than that which we gave him, for his teachers. He also said he needed extra rent money. (In Ghana, you must pay a year of rent up front.) I sacrificed to give him the money, only to find he used it to build a house for himself.

I allowed him to keep his house but took over his orphanage. He was a grad of our Bible School, and we loved him! But Bettye saw him as a frog, in a vision. So we had to let him go, as he had no explanation for his deeds.

DELIVERANCE MEETING

We did have a great crusade in Obuasi, the gold mining city. And later, in another crusade, we found people who needed deliverance. I had prayed for such people in the United States and read about a Baptist pastor who claimed success in such cases. But I had never had a meeting as such. However, I noted that the Ghanian pastors would allow the disturbed people to whirl around or would push them backward, it seemed, in laying their hands on their foreheads, and they would fall down.

Then they would praise God that the demon was cast out! But no demon had been cast out! Also, when the demons would talk through the possessed person, the pastor would laugh! As if it was a show! I don't see that there is ever a time to laugh at a possessed person or a demon. We don't laugh at Satan! He is our enemy!

So I announced that we would have a *deliverance* meeting on Friday night, and anyone who needed prayer should come on that night. There were several ladies, said to have "spiritual marriages" with the juju men (witch doctors). They somehow were never able to get married normally, or they were hindered from having children.

On Friday night, I had the whole congregation stand and renounce any allegiances with the world, the flesh, or the devil! Then I asked them all to swear their allegiance to Jesus Christ, the Son of God, our Savior and Lord. I told them I would pray all night with them, if necessary.

We told the choir and musicians to sing and play only songs about the Blood of Jesus or similar songs about His Lordship. Then, as we prayed for individuals, one at a time, we again asked each one to declare their allegiance to Jesus Christ, as Savior and Lord, and renounce any allegiance with the world, the flesh, or the devil, Satan!

I worked with the ministers and told them not to allow the people to whirl around in circles. But if they did and fell down, I told them to keep them down, so that we could *command* the demons to come out, in the Name of Jesus (Mark 16:17). And they *must* come out!

We prayed and sang and commanded and rejoiced. The Lord gave me great boldness. Some of the ladies (i.e., the demons that were in them), shut their mouths defiantly and kept them shut. I took my right hand and squeezed their cheeks, forcing their mouths open because, many times, the demons came out through their mouths!

I know this sounds fanatical to some of you readers, but I am just reporting to you what happened on the mission field! I never again had a meeting like that to this day! But I will take nothing back! We prayed till about midnight, with several ladies, and one or two men. And there was great rejoicing!

There was no service on Saturday, and Bettye preached on Sunday. When she asked if anyone needed prayer, there was no response! Usually, there were always those who wanted prayer. I asked Pastor Mathew Kwesie, several times after that service, if those ladies ever showed that they yet needed deliverance, and he answered in the negative. He never had any problem with them after that. So I listed about ten points that we learned from that service and made it part of their Bible School instructions on deliverance.

A POEM FOR AFRICA

I recently had a dream of being back in Africa, but I did not know the people and was not able to find their leader. Perhaps this meant there was a question of who was the leader in Africa, Bettye or I. She was drawn to and loved the young children and wanted an orphanage for them. I saw the homeless teenage boys who hung around the marketplace, hoping that someone would hire them for the day! I felt they needed a home. Even in the capital city, Accra, teenage boys and *girls* slept on the streets, open to great danger.

When I think of these things, I am reminded of Jesus, whose heart seemed to be breaking, as He approached His soon to come atonement on the cross, brought about by the refusal of the religious hierarchy of the Jews to even recognize God in their midst, lest they lose their place, like the Cosa Nostra ("our thing") of the mafia, or *Our Thang* of the street gangs.

And Jesus said, "*O Jerusalem, Jerusalem, the one who kills the prophets and stones those who are sent to her! O Jerusalem, how often I wanted to gather your children together, as a hen gathers her chicks under her wings, but you were not willing! See! Your house is left to you desolate; for I say to you, you shall see me no more till you say, 'Blessed is He who comes in the name of the Lord!"* (Mat. 23:37, 38, NKJV).

Africa, with blinding heat and pitch-black nights, cobras and other snakes on the dark roads (yet where I learned I could go out any time of the day, trying to win souls, as a novelty, a *white man in a black world*, as it were, and people would listen [men particularly, as many of the older women did not speak English, the national language, as girls were only recently allowed in the public schools, where they could learn English.]) I say this because there were some with whom we labored and trusted, but, in the end, showed they were only really interested in our money, and not our God.

So I would say, "*Oh, Africa, Africa, how often we tried to gather you together, but you would not.*"

Oh, Africa, Africa! Land of hungry mouths and hungry souls.

Oh, Cape Coast Castle, with your anchor embedded by the huge Atlantic Ocean, where African men and women were captured or bought from enemy tribes by British and perhaps other slave traders.

Oh, Africa, Africa, with the seemingly, lurking spirits of the captured slaves, with moans you can almost hear, at Cape Coast, *of those who did not choose or want to come to America,* unlike many others who *did* and still seek to come to America!

Yes, how often we would have gathered you together, by the Spirit of Jesus and brought you to His loving feet, where you could escape from the all the spirits that haunt you!

Africa, Africa, Africa, land of many animals, sheep, and goats in the streets, of rainforests, beautiful fields, green meadows, from Takoradi to Twifo Praso and the gold mines of Obuasi, AFRICA, with your dancing joy, upon finding Christ Jesus as Savior! Oh, how we hope and pray that your "house will not be left desolate" but that those who were *true* have gone forth to bring many more to the Savior and to establish a Christian nation, despite Islam, deceiving the people.

As I finish this chapter, I received a call from Bishop Matthew (given this title by Apostle Edward J. Anderson, appointed as our successor, as director of the ministry). He told me they have just started a second Bible school in another city. For a while they had a branch in South Africa, but it proved to be too far to continue with it. So we do thank God that there are those who do continue in the faith! Please pray for Ghana.

CHAPTER 12

THEY DIDN'T WANT TO COME HERE

People all over the world want to come to our country. In Africa, many people asked us to help them come to the United States. In those days, it was very difficult to get a visa to the USA. The personnel of the US Embassy seemed to be afraid that people would not be able to support themselves. (Today, the political situation has changed, in that we take in relatives who cannot support themselves, and illegal immigrants who are protected by sanctuary cities, and even terrorists have been taken in, unawares. As I write, a caravan of some 7,000 people are walking from Central America, hoping somehow to be admitted into our country, the United States of America.)

But when we were there, in the 1990s and early 2000s, the question was always asked, "Who is going to support them?" We could only support them for a limited time, if they came as tourists, so it was almost impossible to get a visa, unless you had family members here, who would support you. Today, however, I understand, we take in about one million immigrants per year, not counting thousands of illegals.

What I am saying is that millions of people are clamoring to come to America, but in contrast, centuries ago English and Dutch slave hunters captured Africans, or bought those who had been captured by other tribes, and then chained and crammed them into ships where they suffered terrible abuse, many dying on the ocean journey over here. The rest were then sold into slavery, where they were brutalized, whipped and tortured, if they tried to escape, and many females were raped by their owners to produce more slaves, until there were more than three million slaves in our country.

I have heard people talk about the "race problem." Years ago, I preached in a "border state." An elder of the church said, "We must deal wisely with our Negroes." I was young at the time, so I said nothing. But I don't believe he was talking about dealing wisely for the *good* of "our Negroes!" I think he was saying, "How can we keep them in their place [segregation]?"

What I would say today is *it is not the race problem*, it is *our* problem. We, our white race, brought them here! Of course, they never chose to come here and suffer slavery! It is up to *us* to solve any problem! To my fellow white brothers, I would say, "What are *you* going to do about it? I know there is no easy solution to please everybody. But are you searching, seeking, praying about it?"

Soon after our marriage, I took a job with Illinois Job Service, as a job counselor. A degree was required for the job. Very soon afterward, however, African Americans were *not required* to have a degree (under affirmative action) for that same job. Several secretaries were upgraded to counselors. I never resented it, even though a college education was required for me to get the same job! African Americans deserve any favor they can get! It will never make up for the slavery of their ancestors! (At the same time, for their own sake, they should seek to be self-reliant [or God-reliant] and not rely upon welfare, unless it is necessary.)

Many of you who are reading this may resent and reject it because you are like I was, a white boy, brought up to be patriotic. George Washington was known as the boy who could not tell a lie, who became a great general, defeating even the great British Army, and then became our first president. Thomas Jefferson wrote the Declaration of Independence. But both were slave owners! And probably others of the Continental Congress were slaveholders! We might say they were children of their times. But no matter how you consider it, *slavery is and was wrong*! Although those early planters tried to condone it by the Bible, it was morally wrong!

Apparently, they took Genesis 9:26, 27, "Canaan shall be a servant of Shem," and "of Japheth," to prove that the descendants of Canaan were to be slaves of the Gentiles, but that scripture was fulfilled in Bible times, when the Canaanites were conquered by the Israelites! So there really is *no* scriptural reason to justify slavery! Especially, since many centuries have passed since Noah proclaimed a curse upon his grandson, Canaan. What sense would it make for God to fulfill such a curse four thousand years later?

I must add, however, that Edward Ball tells us that Jefferson's first draft of the Declaration of Independence in June 1776, denounced slavery, blaming King George for the evil, but that passage was rejected by a South Carolina delegate, much to the disappointment of Jefferson (Ball, Edward, *Slaves in the Family*, Ballantine Books, New York, N.Y., 1999, p. 221).

Like most white people, we do not even take time to consider what it is like to be children and grandchildren of slaves, who were suddenly given (freedom?) but *never received the promised "40 acres and a mule!"* I was in my twenties, the first time I heard a black preacher tell us that at least some, if not most white slave owners, took advantage of their female slaves, to satisfy their lusts, and bring more slaves into existence!"

So although a great new nation emerged at that time, and years following, it had two great faults—how slavery was allowed and how the Native Americans were treated. There is some parallel with the way the children of Israel were made slaves in Egypt and the slavery of Africans in America. God called a man named Moses to go and tell Pharaoh, "Let My people go."

If we study history, I believe we also must say that God whispered in the ears of men like John Brown, saying, "Let my people go," who, though his insurrection was unsuccessful and led to his death and that of his sons, and his black followers, yet inevitably, it also led to the Civil War, which by far, took more lives than any other of our country's wars. At least six hundred thousand died, Southerners and Northerners, which may be called a partial atonement for the evil of hundreds of years of slavery, until the issuing of the Emancipation Proclamation by Lincoln in 1863.

This was followed by the Reconstruction Era, immediately following the end of the War in 1865, in which, surprisingly, 10 percent of political offices were filled by ex-slaves! But this movement was countered by Jim Crow Laws and the birth of segregation, with many blacks becoming "sharecroppers," for as long as another century or more, in which they were told by white landowners, at the end of the year, that they made no money but just enough to barely eat and begin another year as farmers with no profit! So their lot in life was little, if any, better than slavery.

My wife, Bettye was well acquainted with this situation, as many of her schoolmates were sharecroppers. Somehow, Bettye's grandfather was able to buy land, which led to pride in her life, which she had to deal with as being a member of the Baker family. Nevertheless, she was so *glad*, at Christmastime for example, to be able to share their food with neighbors, who were not even given an "apple for Christmas" by their landowners, as Bettye often said, in her own words!

So, now let us truly proclaim that all men *are* equal and have the right to pursue happiness, especially through Jesus Christ, our Savior and our God. Let blacks and whites unite in true love for one another, as we are brothers and sisters in Christ. And may there be a new America! A new future!

THE CIVIL RIGHTS MOVEMENT

It happened like this: Dr. Martin Luther King Jr. was born the same year as I, 1929. *But that was about the only thing we had in common. He received his BA degree six years before I did!* And his bachelor of divinity *eight years before I did!* I believe he was a genius, as well as a great spiritual leader! He also received a PhD in Systematic Theology from Boston University in 1955, when I had completed only one year of seminary. It took me years to appreciate his work, and my appreciation seems to be growing, the longer I live.

I remember only four African Americans at Northern Baptist Theological Seminary, where I graduated in 1959. (Although I recently attended Founders Day at their new seminary in Lisle, Illinois, where two African Americans were especially honored, and I estimated the audience of one of the programs as two-thirds African Americans, probably because they now also have a seminary in Chicago. So I was greatly surprised and inspired by such a change in the last half century or so.)

But back in the late fifties, one of my black classmates invited me to a program featuring an up-and-coming Negro minister. But, all I remember about it was a skit in which his wife, or someone who was playing the part, called him "Rev. King," even in private. If it was about civil rights, I missed it! But some ten years later, when Bettye and I were married, her father told her to put a "handle" on my name, i.e., call me Mr. Lythberg. So I assume that was the black custom to show respect for a husband. Incidentally, Bettye never did it. (And I never expected her to do so.)

As a young white man, I heard about J. Edgar Hoover, director of the FBI, whom I respected greatly, accusing King of being a communist. I did not know if it was true or not, but I chose to withhold judgment. Of course, the next few years showed there was no truth in the accusation. Therefore, we would have to say it was only prejudice or racism.

I believe that Hoover, like many other whites of his time, misunderstood the love of God in Dr. King, just as Jesus, Himself, was misunderstood and *rejected* by the spiritual leaders of His day!

King, himself said he had no idea that he would become the leader of a great *effective civil rights movement* when he accepted the pastorate of the Dexter Avenue Baptist Church in 1954. Rosa Parks had taken a seat in the front of a bus in Montgomery, Alabama. She was extremely tired! The segregation rules for buses was that when there were no seats open in the front, White Only section, a Negro would have to give up his or her seat for a white person. But when a white man came to take her seat, expecting her to get up and go to the back of the bus, Mrs. Parks, already a civil rights activist, decided she was "tired" in more ways than one! She decided she was tired of giving in to unjust laws. She just decided not to get up and give her seat to a white man. Of course, that led to her arrest, leading to the Civil Rights Movement, in earnest!

King was elected president of the Montgomery Improvement Association, leading to the bus boycott, the student lunch counter sit-ins in many cities, the Freedom Riders, the encounter with "Bull" Connor and his fire hoses and police dogs seen on national TV in 1963. King was arrested and jailed fourteen times, and twice, bombs were thrown on his porch.

But finally, he would appeal to Presidents John F. Kennedy and Lyndon Johnson. In those interviews, I would say his manner was dignified but respectful. He met them as man-to-man, and they accepted him as such! Later, when Kennedy heard King's "I have a Dream" speech, he said, "He's damn good...Damn good!" (Pardon the language.)

That was on August 28, 1963, as the climax of the March on Washington DC of some 124,000 people. Some said King changed his speech at the end, that he had preached on his "dream" many times before and was advised by his friends not to do it again. But as you listen to him waxing eloquent, another of his friends said, "He is about to 'take them to church.'" I believe no one can doubt that the anointing of God was on his words, some of which were, *"I have a dream that one day on the red hills of Georgia, sons of former slaves and sons of former slave owners will be able to sit down together at the table of brotherhood... I have a dream that my four children will one day live in a nation where they will not be judged by the color of their skin, but by the content of their character...and when we allow freedom to ring, when we let it ring from every village and hamlet, from every state and city, we will be able to speed up the day when all of God's children—black men and white men, Jews and Gentiles,*

Catholics and Protestants—will be able to join hands and to sing in the words of the old Negro spiritual, 'Free at last, free at last, thank God Almighty, we are free at last!'"

Strangely enough, I was in Memphis, Tennessee, preaching a "revival" at the same time Dr. King was marching with six thousand people, protesting low wages and poor conditions for the city's garbage workers, most of whom were African Americans. To my shame, I must say I knew very little about it, except that our meetings were cancelled two nights because of a curfew. I was busy inviting people near the church to the revival meetings.

Little did I know that the following week, Dr. King would be killed by an assassin's bullet. But it seems he almost expected it! In his last sermon, he spurred his followers to go on, but didn't know how long *he* would go on. But he was not concerned because he had "*been to the mountaintop*" (Washington, James M., Editor, *Martin Luther King, Jr., I Have a Dream Writings and Speeches That Changed the World*. Foreword by Coretta Scott King, Harper San Francisco, 2012. P. 203).

But what of his legacy? I will be bold to stress that just as God called Moses to go to Egypt and tell Pharaoh, "*Let my people go!*" So God called Dr. Martin Luther King Jr. to go to presidents and his oppressors and say, "*Let my people go!*" In an age when many are called apostles, let me also say that Dr. King proved himself to be a true Apostle, because that is what apostles do, they preach the powerful and greatly needed truth for their generation, as he did!

It is hard for us to realize what a great movement the *Civil Rights Movement* was! What great victories were won!

June 1956—The US Supreme Court affirmed the ruling of the district court that racial segregation on city bus lines in Birmingham, Alabama was unconstitutional!

September 1957—President Eisenhower federalized the Arkansas National Guard to escort nine African American students into a white high school in Little Rock.

May 1963—The Supreme Court ruled Birmingham segregation unconstitutional.

June 1963—President Kennedy federalized the Alabama National Guard to allow black students to enter the University of Alabama.

August 1965—The Voting Rights Act was signed by President Johnson.

May 1966—Poll tax was ruled unconstitutional by the Supreme Court.

What caused these great victories?

1. It was the *Passive Resistance Nonviolent Movement* that Dr. King adapted from Mahatma Mohandus Ghandi of India.
2. Combined with the insistence by Dr. King that this movement was for the good and the redemption of the white segregationists, as well as the downtrodden Negroes!
3. I don't believe it would have been successful if thousands of African Americans had not "taken up their crosses" (Mark 8:34, 35) and, at least, acted as if they loved their oppressors who jailed and treated many of them roughly.
4. King insisted that they must *love* their segregationist oppressors!

I must confess that I was critical of Dr. King as he attended a "liberal" seminary (Crozer), and I considered that he preached like a modernist, applying the Gospel to the civil rights of Negroes, instead of stressing faith in the atonement of Christ on the cross for the salvation of their souls.

Yet he did preach it in his own way, as he showed, and insisted, that the movement was based on *love*, the agape *love* of God, exhibited by Jesus Christ. I believe there is no way in which the *Civil Rights Movement* could have been successful, if it was not undergirded by this *love* of God in Christ Jesus, accepted by Dr. King!

King taught his followers to love their enemies (the doctrine of Jesus, Mat. 5:43–48, KJV). He convinced gang boys from Chicago to try nonviolence. Their job was to protect the women and children. They did so to the point of catching a brick in midair, thrown against them!

I conclude this tribute to Dr. Martin Luther King Jr. by saying, again, just as certainly as God sent Moses to tell Pharaoh, "Let my people go!" He sent King to organize and lead a mighty army of African Americans and other passive resisters to the political and national and segregationist "Pharaohs," saying *"It is time!"* to let my people go.

We could speak of George Washington Carver, the man who found more than three hundred uses for the peanut; Booker T. Washington of the Tuskegee Institute; Sojourner Truth, of the "underground railroad"; abolitionist Frederick Douglas; to say nothing of literary stars like W. E. B. DuBois, James Baldwin, Richard Wright, Langston Hughes, and many others to show the uncelebrated greatness of African slaves in America, and their children.

But let me mention the athletic field, where we could say, is it not amazing and wonderful that the great grandchildren of slaves, who amount to only 13 percent of our nation's population yet comprise the majority of our NFL football *and* NBA basketball players? We could say a lot more about Branch Rickey and Jackie Robinson, "breaking the color line" in Major League baseball, and Jim Brown and Marion Motley of the Cleveland Browns, doing the same for football.

But having been born and raised in Chicago, I will speak of our beloved Walter Payton and Gayle Sayers, to say nothing of Richard Dent and others of the '85 Champion Bears.

And then we could go to boxing, with the incomparable Joe Louis; the "Sugar Rays," Robinson and Leonard; and of course, Muhammad Ali, to name a few of the "greats."

But now *it is time* to speak of Michelle Alexander and her remarkable, but apparently overlooked book, *The New Jim Crow, Mass Incarceration in the Age of Colorblindness* (The New Press, 120 Wall St. Fl. 31, New York, N. Y. 10005, 2012).

I was active (with churches I attended) in prison ministry, in Chicago; Mobile, Alabama; and Los Angeles, California. Since the prison populations seemed to be predominantly African American, except perhaps, LA, being Hispanics, I assumed that "these were the crooks."

However, after reading Alexander's excellent book, I have come to another conclusion. Rather than going into a "book report" or a lengthy summary of the book, I feel it is very important, in the view of our country, today that I give you my feeling about the book.

1. The population of our prisons *tripled* or *quadrupled* from the 1970s to the 2000s. Prison experts predicted the closing of many prisons! Now, they are overcrowded. Why?

2. The reason is *the War on Drugs* began by President Lyndon Johnson, increased by presidents Clinton and Reagan, insisting on *five-* and *ten*-year sentences for possession of even a few ounces of marijuana, making stings of *SWAT teams* in black neighborhoods for *crack cocaine*, when they would not *dare* to do so for *powder cocaine* in white neighborhoods!

3. Therefore, 85 percent of the prison population is made up of our 13 percent African Americans in the USA, instead of the majority white population, who undoubtedly, use more drugs than the black population, who once arrested, can hardly escape the stigma of *felon*!

4. That is why our prisons are overcrowded by *African Americans*. But not even *African Americans* seem to be disturbed by this injustice, which is a definite hardship of the black population!

5. Something must be done about this malady! But I can't even find African Americans who want to do anything about it, as I write. Was their strength expired by the Civil Right Movement of the last century? African Americans who read this, are you satisfied with the prisons being overcrowded by black and brown people? You must be, because I see many African American politicians on the evening news complaining about many things, but

I haven't heard anyone complaining about the prison situation. Therefore, they are satisfied with the "*New Jim Crow!*"

I will end this chapter with the *national black anthem*, a stirring song, to which we whites should give attention and African Americans *should not forget!*

LIFT EVERY VOICE AND SING

Lift every voice and sing, Till earth and heaven ring. Ring with the harmonies of Liberty. Let our rejoicing rise, High as the list'ning skies. Let it resound, loud as the rolling sea. Sing a song full of the faith that the dark past has taught us; Sing a song, full of the hope that the present has brought us. Facing the rising sun of our new day begun. Let us march on till victory is won. Stony the road we trod, Bitter the chastening rod, Felt In the days when hope unborn has died: Yet with a steady beat, have not our weary feet come to the place for which our fathers sighed? We have come over a way that with tears has been watered: We have come, treading our path through the blood of the slaughtered. Out of our gloomy past, till now we stand at last, where the white gleam of our bright star is cast.

God of our weary years, God of our silent tears.
Thou hast brought us thus far on the way; Thou hast by Thy might, led us into the light, keep us forever in the path, we pray, Lest our feet stray from the places, our God, where we met Thee, Lest our hearts, drunk with the wine of the world, we forget Thee; Shadowed beneath Thy hand, May we forever stand, True to our God, True to our native land.

CHAPTER 13

BETTYE'S LAST DAYS

Bettye was seventy-two years of age when we moved to Bourbonnais, near Kankakee, Illinois, because we had two daughters and several grandchildren there, particularly our youngest, Rebecca and her two daughters, Jaylenn, almost seven years old, and Jacen, almost five. It was the summer of 2008.

We spent a day in mid-August in a nearby park, which bordered the Kankakee River. Bettye said she walked a total of four miles, as we explored the park, with the girls.

She was having some physical problems, so a week or two later, we went for a checkup with Dr. Paul Chemello. We had gotten to know him very well in recent years. In fact, when Bettye had gained weight to over two hundred pounds, he said to her, as he tells his mother, "There is just more of you to love." He and I also had some good discussions about "religion," which he appreciated. But he became very alarmed when her tests showed her oxygen level as very low. He advised us that she needed to go to the hospital to check out her condition. I said I would take her there. He said, "No, I will call for an ambulance, so she will be served as soon as possible."

Little did we realize at that time, she would spend most of the rest of the year in hospitals and a nursing home!

They took her to St. James Hospital in Olympia Fields, Illinois. A day or two later, they discovered the artery to her kidney was 80 percent blocked. So a splint was inserted to keep the artery open. At the time, I did not realize the serious nature of the surgery. They had taken her out of her hospital room for tests. Finally, they called me on the phone in her room and asked me to sign for my approval of the surgery. I did so, of course, because the operation was said to be necessary.

It was already late in the afternoon. (Later, we realized that the lateness of the hour may have been a factor of a tired surgeon, who made *two* cuts in Bettye's groin, but only one was sealed off, causing her abdomen to fill with blood, "flattening the bladder, like a pancake," we were told, days later, when it was discovered in emergency surgery!)

But after a day or two, she was discharged to go home. (It happened to be my birthday, August 31.) But it was not happy for Bettye! The next day, she was in *excruciating pain* and was also unable to urinate! Someone might ask, "Why didn't you pray?" Well, of course, we prayed—and you know of the many miracles God did in Bettye's life, particularly. I prayed for a miracle healing for her, practically every day she lived, until the day she died, and went to be with our Lord (Phil. 1:21, 23; 2 Cor. 5:8). But we Christians are not immune from the trials of this life. In fact, we must realize that our sojourn on this earth *is a trial.* One day, we shall all be judged, whether for heaven or hell (Heb. 9:27) or concerning our faithfulness in living for Christ. But why God does not always heal is a mystery left with Him, as has been said, even "healers" die.

So I took her to a local hospital. But all they could do was to give her morphine for the pain and send her back to St. James Hospital in Olympia Fields (about twenty miles away). The next day she was taken for emergency surgery. Thank God for Dr. Eugene Tanquilot, a Christian doctor, who told us about the two cuts that had been made by the previous surgeon.

The pain and inability to urinate was because of a large *hematoma* (collection of blood) oppressing her bladder and other organs. During that night her kidneys failed, causing them to fear that she was dying, but, no doubt *miraculously,* her kidneys came back to life! (Later, three doctors and a nurse told us they had not expected her to live through the night!) God was not ready for her yet!

It was a long, slow process for her to regain a measure of health. I was with her every day, all day, and sometimes stayed overnight with my son, David, who was then married and lived in Homewood, near the hospital.

We felt that it was only right to sue the hospital or the surgeon who made the two cuts in the light of the suffering she went through and her eventual death, almost one year ago, as I write in 2017. However, we contacted five law offices, and none of them would take the case, probably because the medical records made no mention of the second cut, causing the hematoma. But the emergency surgeon said he was willing to testify as to the second unsealed cut.

But we put it all in God's hands and were not bitter about it, although she continued to suffer. On October 16, 2008, Bettye was ambulanced to Provena Nursing Home in Kankakee for rehabilitation. For the next eight years, she would have several more stays in nursing homes.

For some time, she recovered sufficiently to walk outside and at the mall but also had many trips to hospitals, as well as the nursing homes. We had nurses coming regularly to our home. Finally, her kidneys regressed to the point she was taken to dialysis centers for three or four years, three times a week. She complained very little but was generally very quiet after three hours on the dialysis machines and had little appetite. It was very hard on her.

Many times, I called her my "soldier," she took her lot in life so valiantly. We joined a small church called the "Horn of Oil," in downtown, Kankakee. It got to the place where Bettye longed to go "home," to "cross the Jordan River," and be with her Lord. She felt she did little good on this earth anymore, but the pastor and his wife and the people of the church were so nice, often bringing us food. And the worship services were so anointed that she enjoyed it every time I was able to bring her. Once, she even spoke at a women's luncheon from a sitting position. My poor darling had to suffer so much! *But to God be the glory!* I believe we had some of the best days of our marriage, as I finally retired after more than fifteen years as a substitute school teacher to become her full-time *caregiver.*

Bettye was hospitalized three times for an arrhythmic heartbeat, with her heart alternating from fast to slow beats, as it was too weak to beat regularly, but beat fast, trying to catch up and slow when the organ tired out. (At least, that was the way I understood it.) Finally, she had good care at Christ Hospital in Oak Lawn, Illinois. But when she recovered somewhat, they would not let her go home with me, as I was too old to take care of her. They insisted she must go to a nursing home for rehab.

The problem was the only home we could find with an opening was old fashioned. (They still had beds that were raised and lowered by a hand-crank, no electricity.) We felt we had no other choice, so left her there for the night.

Our daughter, Mickey, could not sleep that night, thinking about her mother in that subpar nursing home. She called, saying we had to take her out of there. I had come to the same conclusion, so early in the morning, I went there.

I told them I was taking my wife home. They told me I would have to get the approval of the whole "team." While I was talking to them, Bettye came up to us in a wheelchair. She was pleasantly surprised to see me! When I complained about the hand cranks for the beds, they began to tell me about all the improvements they were going to make. It was only a matter of time.

But by this time, they saw that I "meant business." They asked, "Who is going to take care of her?" I was about eighty-five years old at the time, but I said, "*I will take care of her.*" Bettye was sitting there in a wheelchair, and I know she was glad to hear me say this, so confidently.

Finally, the "team" said, "We must get your doctor's approval, to let you take her home." So they called Dr. Abraham, and he approved! Praise God! I got her out of there in record time! She was *so* glad to be home! This was one time I "scored a lot of points" with Bettye!

And it was the beginning of a new "walk" in my life. You may remember that after the Last Supper, when Jesus faced the cross, *His purpose for coming into the world, He wrapped himself in a towel and washed the feet of each of His disciples* (John 13:3–17). He said He did this as an example. That they should wash one another's feet—in other words, be willing to do the work of a servant. He said, if you want to be *first*, then be *last*. If you have ambition to be the greatest Christian, that ambition is good. But the way to be first and the greatest is *to be servant of all!*

So now I became a servant, I would no longer fret or worry if I could not do what I wanted to do, such as work on my memoirs, as I do now. Bettye would say, "Why are you always writing?" From that point on, Bettye became *first*. (Of course, she was second to God. But I know the Lord was telling me to make her *first* in my doings. That way, I was making God and His will for my life *first*. So now I had peace. I had no conflict about it. If she wanted my time, my presence, my companionship, I stopped anything and everything to be with her. I was there for her!)

Let me say here that the call to be a servant, as Jesus illustrated and modeled it, is the *highest calling* of God—to be servant to all, as Mother Teresa did to the lowest. And as already mentioned, Dr. King's program and plan was successful because he insisted on *loving* his oppressors! And behind it all was the love of God, our Savior Jesus Christ. We will not be successful, in the end, white or black, unless we follow the example of our Savior and Dr. King. The challenge is for all of us to accept this high calling!

Did I do this servanthood perfectly? No, probably not. But I had made the decision to do so and was at peace with it. It was all in God's hands. I enjoyed a peace I had not had before! I began taking Bettye to dialysis and back by myself, as she did not like to wait if her transportation was late, as often happened. So began the most precious part of our married life. We grew very close, although she soon began to suffer more and more.

Bettye now weighed as much as 250 pounds, and I am not a big man, my weight went down to 135, so I got free gym workouts from my health insurance and tried hard to build up so I could carry her because she began to fall more and more, and I could not lift her up again by myself.

In the last two years of her life, our son, David, and I took Bettye twice to Baton Rouge, Louisiana, to attend the Family Worship Center of Evangelist Jimmy Swaggart, the last time being the *Resurrection Camp Meeting*. We met the Swaggarts and some of their Bible College teachers prayed for her. She enjoyed it very much! But she had to take her dialysis there, too.

Both times she fell and hurt her legs along the way, but she did not complain. In her last hospital stay, the dialysis technician could withdraw very little fluid from her, despite spending two or three hours at it. We (our children and I) had two discussions with the head nurse, and we reluctantly allowed Bettye to be taken to a hospice for her last days.

She had stopped talking to us but was treated very well by the nurses, doctor, and other workers. When she was restless, they gave her morphine under her tongue. She lasted five days and was taken home by her Lord on Friday, November 13, 2016, almost one year ago, as I write.

Bettye had a glorious homegoing service (funeral) under our pastor, James Carr. There was great rejoicing, and one of our great granddaughters responded to the invitation to accept Christ as her Savior, also!

Several months before leaving this earth, she announced (especially to David, our only son, whom she seemed to see as her little boy, at that time) that she would be leaving soon. It was a very special spiritual moment.

Our marriage, on this earth, chaotic, though it started, lasted almost forty-seven years but was better and more beautiful, at the end, than at the beginning!

So I say to Bettye, my darling wife, "*God be with you till we meet again, at Jesus feet, in Heaven!*"

EPILOGUE

TO YOUR HEALTH!

There are just two main things I want to tell you—(1) If you are a Christian, *your body does not belong to you!* It is the temple of the Holy Spirit (2 Cor. 6:16, KJV). Therefore, since God lives in you (and me) we ought to take the best care we can of this temple (our bodies, of which God says, we are "fearfully and wonderfully made" [Psalm 139:14, NKJV]). That means it is our duty as stewards and servants of God to take good care of these wonderful bodies He has given us. Of course, I know that some people are born with or soon fall prey to certain afflictions. For these, may we all pray that they may be healed and made whole by our healing God, whose Son died for our afflictions, as well as our sins (Mat. 8:16, 17; Isa. 53:5).

(2) *The most important meal of your day is breakfast!* Very few overweight people eat breakfast. Therefore, they may be hungry and fall prey to fattening or junk food during the day. It is appalling to see so many overweight people *and* underweight, skinny people. I know that, in many cases, it is the result of diseases or bodily imbalances, but God has generally given us very beautiful and efficient bodies. But sometimes, we dissipate or otherwise abuse our bodies. *Why?*

Could it be that we do not *respect ourselves* enough to take care of the bodies which God has given us, but expects us to maintain? Or do we not respect God, who gave us these bodies?

In my youthful years, I wanted to improve my health, by exercise and proper food, for selfish reasons. And I suppose that is true of most of us. As I have said, I weighed only ninety pounds, beginning my senior year in high school. My greatest ambition had been to be an athlete. But that dream seemed impossible as I found myself seeking God and reading the Bible. I did find Him, or rather, He found me, as I have explained about my conversion experience.

But what I want to say now is that our seeking to lose weight, or gain weight, or improve our physiques, should be *for the glory of God*, as all our living should be for Him. I did not realize that as a young Christian, but now, in old age, I do.

When we lived in Dallas, Texas, in the early 1990s, a restaurant owner, turned chiropractor, told us two important things. (1) You must "*move the bones*" to be healthy, and (2) You should eat a piece or two of fruit for breakfast. Well, I eat whole grain breakfast foods, and even if it is raisin bran, I add extra raisins and then try to add a piece of fruit, usually a sliced banana or peach, etc. For many years, I tried to use what I called powdered vegetables to increase the fiber in my diet, but now God has blessed me so I do not need to do so.

I thank God, I am never constipated, neither do I have any stomachaches or digestive problems or heartburn. But if I did, I would roll my abdominal muscles (to be explained later) and other exercises, and then, drink water.

Your daily food is important. Notice, we do not use the word *diet* because you do not need to go on "diets." You need only to adopt a healthy lifestyle, if you are over- or underweight. I see no reason to eat *pasta or starches*, except a small amount, perhaps, to make the food taste better.

Meat, vegetables, and fruits (with a little dairy products) are what I concentrate on. I love cookies, cakes, and all kinds of desserts, especially ice cream, but I eat almost none of the above, (although health experts tell us that carbohydrates and some fats are necessary). Your body needs very little of those sweets mentioned, to say nothing about soda pop, with its sugar, which becomes *fat*, if not needed for energy!

I should also say that because I had a "nervous stomach" in my teen ages, I was told to chew my food until it disappeared (was swallowed). Because of this, it usually takes me a little longer to eat my meals than most people.

Just as important as the food you eat, and probably even more important, is *exercise!* I believe the very best exercise is weight-bearing exercise, commonly called weightlifting. The purpose of it is to normalize the body, to add strength and lean muscle mass to your body, or if overweight, to gradually sweat off the extra pounds.

Bob Hoffman, Olympic coach, head of the York Barbell Company of York, Pennsylvania, and editor of *Strength and Health* magazine, used to say, "A task which does not try your strength is sure to weaken it at length." That is the way God made it! Despite Solomon's poem of the falling short of our bodies in old age (Eccles. 12:1–7), I have found better health than in earlier years, at eighty- eight years of age! I am forced to conclude that *our God made these wonderful bodies to prosper!* (1 John:2) *if we are not afraid of hard work*! But everything must be done "decently and in order" (1 Cor. 14:40), i.e., you must *gradually* increase the resistance (the weights you use).

I am not such a good example of it, as I weigh only about 145 pounds at about five feet, eight inches tall. But I am still going, at my age. I am an underachiever, still trying to do as much as I can. Presently, I work out in a gym every day, for an hour or so, doing upper body one day and lower body the other day. I do six or seven sets of each exercise (even ten sets on the leg press), using as much weight as I can, while I never did more than three sets until this last year or two. And I have more energy than a few years ago. I also have not had a cold (my lifetime downfall) for several years. I suffered from rhinitis, a chronic blowing of the nose, causing nose bleeding and allergies, which are now gone, *praise our great God! I give him all the praise and credit*! For I know that I can do nothing without Him (John 15:5).

I also jog around the gym and walk one day for the heart, which is most important.

You can also do calisthenics—pushups, sit-ups, leg raises, deep-knee bends, etc., and that might be a way to get started. Somehow, I also learned to roll my stomach (i.e., the abdominal muscles) from watching another boy do it, and later reading about it in *Strength and Health* magazines. You can roll the muscles up and down—start by pulling the lower muscles in, and gradually working up, then reverse the procedure. It is a good thing to do, if you are constipated or have a stomachache. The rolling of your abdominal muscles is like an internal massage for your internal organs. Another good exercise is to pull your abdominal muscles in as far as you can and then relax. I like to do fifty repetitions, maybe twice, if I have time. (But you must work up to that gradually.) You can do it standing in lines at stores or waiting in a doctor's office. I have watched people to see if anyone notices I am doing it, and no one ever does! Believe me! People are too interested in their own business to notice.

My father had a book about exercise; it must have been a hundred years old! It told about a very important exercise. Sitting in a chair, you pull your waist in and then make circles with your waist, from one side to the other, forty in one direction and forty the opposite way. But it is more beneficial to do it down on your knees, like a dog. (It is hard to explain it without pictures.) These exercises are all good for your internal organs.

One last procedure, which is very important for your posture, which is vital—you *imagine* that there is a big balloon up in the air, and it is attached to your sternum and is bearing up 50 percent of your weight! That way, you will keep your head and shoulders up and back where they should be for good posture. Most people, like me have one leg slightly longer than the other. Instead of swaying from side to side, I find myself walking only on the ball of the foot on my shorter leg, with the heel barely touching the ground, as I imagine myself borne up by the balloon attached to the sternum bone, in the middle of my chest, and I walk with good posture, instead of swaying from side to side.

In closing, I will repeat the few pointers my father gave me: "*If you mean to do a thing, and mean to do it, really, never let it be by halves, but do it fully, freely.*"

These next two he said, perhaps, because he was a semipro boxer and had to make weight at 133 pounds, as a lightweight (although he was taller than me at 5'11", built like a triangle), he said, "*The whiter the bread, the sooner you're dead!*" And "*The best exercise is pushing yourself away from the table.* (You should always feel as though you could eat a little more, as you leave the table.)

Like a preacher, I close again. One last thing: they used to say, "Good night! *Sleep tight!* Don't let the bedbugs bite!" But "*sleep tight!*" is just what you *do not* want to do. I suppose they said that in the days they let the coal fires burn out, and you would be without heat on a cold, winter night. Nowadays, most of us can leave the gas or electric heat on at night.

What you want to do is *sleep loose!* Loosen up your back (spinal cord). I generally pull my two legs up and to the right and then to the left, until I hear at least one "crack" in my back. Remember, *move the bones.* Do whatever you must do, rotate your back like the football players do to relax before going to bed, if necessary.

And then, spiritual help. For years I have been repeating Isaiah 26:3 as I lay, usually on my right side, to put me to sleep. Thank God, it works about 90 percent of the time. "*You will keep him in perfect peace, whose mind is stayed on You, because he trusts in You*" (NKJV). *To your health!*

CONCLUSION

TO YOUR ETERNITY!

Thank you for reading my story! I hope it has been a help to you. If you have not yet accepted the Lord Jesus Christ as your Savior, I invite and urge you to do so, repenting of your sins—for He is the One who died on the cross, as the sacrifice for our sins, as we are all sinners (Rom 3:23, KJV). He will give you Eternal Life in the New Jerusalem, coming down from Heaven to earth, so you can live with God, forever (Rev. 21:1–8; 22:12–21, KJV).

Let's face it. There are two kinds of people in the world—converted and unconverted. Twice born (John 3:3, 7, KJV) and once-born. Christians and non-Christians. If you are a Christian, the Bible calls you a saint (sanctified or set apart person, holy, given to God).

Those who are not saved are called *sinners* (Gal. 2:15, KJV). But Christians sin, too, possibly every day, as we do not know our own thoughts and attitudes. As Jesus said, "Whoever looks at a woman to lust for her has already committed adultery with her in his heart" (Mat. 5:28, NKJV). If you have evil, jealous, envious thoughts against another human being, you have killed him or her in your heart (Exodus 20:13, KJV).

Of course, then, if you are a racist, with superior thoughts about yourself and your race, and evil thoughts, even condescending or "parental" thoughts about those of another race, you are a sinner! The difference between a sinner and a Christian is *not* that one is a sinner and the other is not, but that a truly Born-Again Christian does not *want* to sin! Yet as we are told in 1 Corinthians. 7:15, 18, 19 (NKJV), even Paul, the apostle, did what he did not want to do (through temptations, no doubt) but found himself unable to do what he wanted to do and was supposed to do!

Therefore, what should a Christian do? He or she must "die to self" (John 12:24) and take up his cross, which even Jesus struggled to do, after being "purged (whipped thirty-nine times, with glass and metal in the whip, which could cut into the skin, muscles and bones, and even cause death).

Taking up our cross is *not* suffering for our own *sins and selfish failures* but suffering *because we are Christians* and are hated and opposed for such, as the family of a Christian, whose tongue was cut out of his mouth by Muslims, forgave them, saying "we are the people who love."

Secondly, if you want to follow Jesus and be the greatest and excel, become a *servant to all*! (That is, all people, high and low, sinners and saints.)

If you are not sure you are saved, pray a prayer like this, "Dear God, I know that I am a sinner, and have done things that are wrong and against Your Holy Law. But I believe that Jesus died on the cross, taking the penalty for my sins! So, Lord Jesus, come into my heart, take away all my sins, and I will serve You with all my heart, mind, and soul!

"Thank You, Lord, for coming into my heart. I will read and study Your Word, attend a church that teaches these things, and will tell others about You! Amen!"

God bless you all!

BIBLIOGRAPHY

Alexander, Michelle. 1999. *The New Jim Crow, Incarceration in the Age of Colorblindness*. The New Press.
Ball, Edward. 2014. *Slaves in the Family*. New York Ballantine Publishing Group.
Brown, Rebecca. 1992. *Prepare for War*. New Kensington, Pennsylvania: Whitacker House.
Coleman, Robert E. 1996. *The Master Plan of Evangelism*, Second Edition, Abridged. Grand Rapids, Michigan: Fleming H. Revell.
Colson, Charles and James Stuart Bell. 1984. *Lies That Go Unchallenged in Popular Culture*. Wheaton, Illinois: Tyndale House Publishers.
Dengler, Sandy. 1987. *Susanna Wesley, Servant of God*. Chicago: Moody Press.
Fenelon, Francois. 1973. *Let Go, to Get Peace and Real Joy*. New Kensington, Pennsylvania: Whitaker House.
Fenelon, Francois. 1982. *The Royal Way of the Cross*, edited by H. Helms. Brewster, Massachusetts: Paraclete Press.
Finney, Charles. 2000. *Power from God*. New Kensington, Pennsylvania: Whitacker House.
Finney, Charles G. 1994. *Finney's Systematic Theology, New Expanded Edition*, edited by D. Carroll, B. Nicely and L. G. Parkhurst Jr.) Bloomington, Minnesota: Bethany House Publishers.
Guyon, Madame. 1982. *Experiencing God through Prayer*. Kensington, Pennsylvania: Whitacker House.
Harley, Willard F. Jr. 2007. *His Needs, Her Needs, Building an Affair-Proof Marriage*. Grand Rapids: Michigan: Fleming H. Revell.

Hayes, Dan. 1995. *Fireseeds of Spiritual Awakening*, revised edition. Orlando, Florida: Campus Crusade for Christ, Integrated Resources.

Hunter, Charles and Frances Hunter. 1983. *To Heal the Sick*. Kingwood, Texas: Hunter Books.

Ilibagiza, Immaculée and Steve Irwin. 2006. *Left To Tell, Discovering God Amidst the Rwandan Holocauast*. Hay House, Inc.

King, Martin L. Jr. n.d. *A Time to Break Silence, Essential Works of Martin Luther King, Jr. for Students*. Boston: Beacon Press

Kessler, Jay and Joe Musser. 1989. *Restoring a Loving Marriage*. Elgin: Illinois: David Cook Publishing Company.

Kinnear, Angus, 1980. *The Story of Watchman Nee, Against the Tide*. Wheaton, Illinois: Tyndale House Publishers Inc.

Lutzer, Erwin W. 2006. *The DaVinci Deception*, TBN edition. Carol Stream, Illinois: Living Books (Tyndale House Publishers Inc.).

McBirnie, William S. 2004. *The Search for the Twelve Apostles*, Special TBN edition. Carol Stream, Illinois: Tyndale House Publishers.

Pusey, E. B., translator. 2003. *The Confessions of Saint Augustine*. New York: Barnes and Noble Books.

Washington, James M., ed. 1992. *Martin Luther King Jr., I Have a Dream, Writings and Speeches That Changed the World*. San Francisco: Harper Collins.

Wilkinson, Bruce. 1982. *Secrets of the Vine, Course Workbook*. Global Vision Resources.

Woolsey, Jim. 2015. *Passport to the Impossible, a Missionary's Incredible Journey with God*. Baton Rouge: Louisiana: Jimmy Swaggart Minisrtries.

Wubbells, Lance, compiler and editor. 2002. *A 30-Day Devotional Treasury, R. A. Torrey, Holy Spirit*. Lynwood, Washington: Emerald Books.

Yohannan, K. P. 2004. *Revolution in World Missions, One Man's Journey to Change a Generation*. GFA Books, a Division of Gospel for Asia.

You may order books by writing to Lythberg Books, PO Box 224, Bourbonnais, Ilinois 60914, or from Amazon.com.

Books by Bettye Y. Lythberg:

Through Much Tribulation We Shall Overcome, Don't Give Up ($10.00)

Gold Tried By Fire ($7.00) (Shipping and Handling, this book only, $.75 & for all other books listed are $1.50)

Other Books by Richard W. Lythberg:

Is Allah the God of the Bible? A Comparison of Islam and Christianity ($9.95)

(Also may be ordered from Infinity Publishing by calling toll free 877 [buy book])

Men's Manual for Holiness, With Particular Reference To Sexual Purity ($10.00)

Please add $1.50 for shipping and handling, for each book.
THANK YOU AND MAY GOD BLESS YOU ALL!

ABOUT THE AUTHOR

Richard Wesley Lythberg, Wheaton College, 1953

Richard Wesley Lythberg lives with his son in Bourbonnais, Illinois, near his three daughters and other relatives. The author spends his time exercising in a gym and studying for possible further writing.

CPSIA information can be obtained
at www.ICGtesting.com
Printed in the USA
JSHW011117261119
2644JS00004B/57